TO UNDERSTAND THE BIBLE LOOK FOR JESUS

TO UNDERSTAND THE BIBLE LOOK FOR JESUS

THE BIBLE STUDENT'S GUIDE TO THE BIBLE'S CENTRAL THEME

NORMAN GEISLER

BAKER BOOK HOUSE
Grand Rapids, Michigan

PHOTOLITHOPRINTED BY CUSHING - MALLOY, INC.
ANN ARBOR, MICHIGAN, UNITED STATES OF AMERICA

CONTENTS

PREFACE

This book grows out of the conviction that Christ is the key to the interpretation of the Bible, not only in that He is the fulfillment of Old Testament types and prophecies, but in that Christ is the thematic unity of the whole span of scriptural revelation. Christ claimed on several occasions to be the central message of the whole sweep of Old Testament Scripture (Luke 24:27, 44; John 5:39; Heb. 10:7; Matt. 5:17). This work is an attempt to take seriously the affirmation of Christ who said, "Everything written about me in the law of Moses and the prophets and the psalms must be fulfilled" (Luke 24:44).

The Christ-centered approach to the Bible in these pages is not centered primarily in a study of the types, or even of the prophecies of the Old Testament, but rather it is an attempt to see Christ as the unity and unfolding message of the whole of Sacred Writ. Christ is presented as the tie between the Testaments, the content of the whole canon, and the unifying theme within each book of the Bible.

The emphasis here is upon the Christological unity of the Bible as it relates to the great sections and structure of Scripture. In a sense, this is a Christ-centered survey of the Bible.

There is no direct theological purpose of this book, but it does address theological questions, such as the inspiration of the Bible and the deity of Christ. However, these grow out of or relate to the central theme of the presentation of Christ as the clue to a correct interpretation of the Bible.

Other than the central thrust of this book, which is to suggest some Christ-centered approaches to the Scriptures, perhaps the most important question addressed is that of the relationship between Christ and Scripture as revelations of

God. It is contended here that the purpose of the propositional revelation of the Scripture is to present the person of
the Saviour; the Bible is the instrument of God to convey the
message of Christ and, therefore, the Bible should not be
sought so much for its own sake, but should be searched for
the purpose of finding Christ, for "to him all the prophets
bear witness" (Acts 10:43).

1

CHRIST IS THE KEY TO THE BIBLE

CHRIST: THE KEY TO THE BIBLE'S INSPIRATION

The authority and integrity of Christ is at stake in the question of the Bible's inspiration. If the Bible is not the very Word of God, final and unbreakable, as Jesus claimed that it was, then one cannot place confidence in one of the central theological assertions of Christ, For it is beyond question that the Christ of the New Testament Gospels had, as one of the central emphases of His ministry, the categorical assertion of the divine authority of the Old Testament. And what Jesus claimed for the Old Testament, He promised for the New Testament.

CHRIST'S CLAIMS ABOUT THE INSPIRATION OF THE OLD TESTAMENT

In Jesus' day there were several ways of referring to the Old Testament as a whole, and most of these were employed by Jesus in affirming the divine inspiration of these sacred writings.

THE SCRIPTURES

Probably the most common way of referring to the Old Testament was to call them the "Scriptures." This term is used fifty times in the New Testament and takes on a technical meaning. In II Timothy 3:16, we read, "All scripture is *inspired* by God," and with this definition the rest of the New Testament concurs. The Scriptures are called "sacred" (II Tim. 3:15), and acknowledged to be the divine rule for human faith and practice (Rom. 15:4; II Tim. 3:16-17).

In this latter regard, Jesus' use of the Scriptures is very instructive. He challenged the religious leaders (Pharisees) of His day, asking, "Have you never read in the *scriptures* . . .?" (Matt. 21:42). To the question of the Sadducees, He replied, "You are wrong, because you know neither the *scriptures* nor the power of God" (Matt. 22:29). Jesus often referred to the necessity of the Scriptures being fulfilled (cf. Matt. 26:54, 56; John 13:18; 17:12). In Luke 24:44 Jesus affirmed that everything written about Himself in the Scriptures "must be fulfilled" (cf. v. 45). On numerous occasions, Christ used the word Scripture in the singular, without citing a specific passage from the Old Testament (cf. John 7:38, 42; 19:36; 20:9). Thus He used the phrase "as the scriptures say" in a somewhat similar fashion to the current expression "as the Bible says."

The Scriptures, for Jesus, were the definitive, divine disclosure to man. He said, "*Scripture* cannot be broken" (John 10:35). Such was the divine authority of the Old Testament writings for Christ—writings which were the rule of faith, which must be fulfilled, and which could not be broken.

IT IS WRITTEN

Closely allied with the word Scriptures is the phrase "it is written," a phrase often used by Jesus to support the divine authority of His teaching. This phrase occurs some ninety-two times in the New Testament. It usually refers to a given passage; sometimes, however, the phrase takes on a broader significance and points to the Old Testament generally. For example, Jesus said, "How is it *written* of the Son of man, that he should suffer many things and be treated with contempt?" (Mark 9:12). He probably is not referring here to a specific passage of the Old Testament but to a theme found throughout the Old Testament (cf. Gen. 3:15; Ps. 22; Isa. 53). On another occasion Jesus said, "*Everything that is written* of the Son of man by the prophets will be accomplished" (Luke 18:31). Here the general nature of the phrase is quite clear. In Luke 21:22, He said, "For these are the days of vengeance, to fulfil *all that is written.*"

Besides these general references to the Old Testament under the phrase "it is written," there are numerous individual citations which reveal that Jesus affirmed an authoritative collection of writings, divine in origin, and unimpeachable in their declarations. Compare, for example, the fact that (1) Jesus resisted Satan by three emphatic quotations of the Old Testament prefaced by *"it is written"* (Matt. 4:4, 7, 10). (2) Jesus cleansed the temple on the authority that *"It is written,* 'My house shall be called a house of prayer'" (Matt. 21:13). (3) He pronounced a woe on His betrayer, based on the fact that "it is written" (Matt. 26:24). (4) Jesus rebuked religious hypocrisy, with "as *it is written*" (quoting Isa. 29:13 in Mark 7:6). (5) He affirmed His own Messiahship from "the place *where it was written,* 'The Spirit of the Lord is upon me . . .'" (Luke 4:17-18). (6) Jesus answered the lawyer's question on how to inherit eternal life by saying, "*What is written* in the law?" (Luke 10:26). (7) He based His own authority and identity with God on the basis of the fact that "*it is written* in the prophets" (John 6:45; cf. 10:34). (8) Jesus even affirmed the authority of what was *written* (in the Old Testament) despite the fact that the religious authorities of His day wished to kill Him for it (cf. Luke 20:16-17).

THAT IT MIGHT BE FULFILLED

Another expression used by Jesus to refer to the authority of the Old Testament as a whole was "that it might be fulfilled." This is found thirty-three times in the New Testament. Although this statement is usually used to cite a given passage of the Old Testament, it is sometimes used in a more general way of the Old Testament as a whole. A good example of the latter comes from the Sermon on the Mount (Matt. 5:17), where Jesus said, "I have come not to abolish them [the Law and the Prophets], *but to fulfil them.*" After His resurrection, Christ made a similar assertion that the

Law, Prophets, and Psalms "must be *fulfilled*" concerning Him (Luke 24:44). In Luke 21:22 Jesus looks to the future when "all that is written" *will be fulfilled*. In the gospel of Matthew alone this expression is used fifteen times. Jesus said He was baptized to *fulfill* all righteousness (Matt. 3:15); He came into this world to *fulfill* the Law and the Prophets, and He must die, otherwise "how then should the scriptures *be fulfilled*, that it must be so?" (Matt. 26:54).

THE LAW

The word *Law* is usually reserved for the first five books of the Old Testament, containing the law of Moses (cf. Luke 2:22; John 1:45). Sometimes, however, it refers to the whole Old Testament. In Matthew 5:18, for instance, Jesus said, "For truly, I say to you, till heaven and earth pass away, not an iota, not a dot, will pass from *the law* until all is accomplished." Not only does Jesus here clearly declare the final authority of the Law but He plainly identifies the "Law" with the "law and the prophets" (v. 17), that is, the entire Old Testament Scriptures are referred to simply as Law. There are other passages in which Christ asserts a divine authority for the Old Testament as the Law of God generally. In John 10:34, for example, Jesus said to the Jews, "Is it not written in your *law?*" having quoted Psalm 82:6 to them. Here the word Law is inclusive of the book of Psalms. Elsewhere, there are similar references by Jesus to "their law" (the Jew's, John 15:25). Likewise, others in New Testament times spoke of the Old Testament as the *Law* of the Jews (cf. Acts 25:8; John 18:31; John 12:34).

THE LAW AND THE PROPHETS

One of the most common names for the Old Testament was "the Law and the Prophets." This phrase occurs about a dozen times in the New Testament. Jesus considered the "Law and Prophets" (1) to be the embodiment of true morality (Matt. 7:12), (2) to indicate the entire compass of the

Old Testament canon of Scriptures (Matt. 11:13), (3) and
as that which He came to fulfill (Matt. 5:17).

WORD OF GOD

Another phrase which reflects the complete authority of
the Old Testament Scriptures is "the Word of God." The
New Testament uses this title several times of the whole Old
Testament. In Romans 9:6, for example, Paul says, "Not as
though the *word of God* had failed"; Hebrews 4:12 affirms
that the "*word of God* is living and active" (cf. also II Cor.
4:2; Rev. 1:2). In John 10:35, Jesus, using the "word of God"
in parallel with the "scripture," affirmed that it "cannot be
broken." Mark 7:13 is even more emphatic, for here Jesus
makes a clear distinction between the "tradition" of the Jews
and "the word of God." Jesus charged them, saying, "So, for
the sake of your tradition, you have made void the *word of
God*" (Matt. 15:6).

The above survey can leave no doubt that the Jesus of the
Gospels affirmed over and over again, as one of the central
emphases of His ministry, that the sacred writings of the
Jewish Old Testament, designated as "Scriptures," "Law,"
"Law and Prophets," were the unbreakable, imperishable and
unimpeachable "Word of God." Christ is the key to the inspiration of the Old Testament since He unquestionably affirmed it; one cannot assail the authority of the Old Testament without impugning the integrity of Christ.

CHRIST'S PROMISE ABOUT THE INSPIRATION OF THE NEW TESTAMENT

The divine authority which Jesus claimed for the Old Testament He also promised for the New Testament. On several
occasions Jesus promised His disciples that after His de-
parture (ascension) the Holy Spirit would guide them in
their utterances about Him. The New Testament Scriptures
are a fulfillment of these promises. It is in this sense that
Christ is also the key to the inspiration of the New Testament.

THE PROMISE OF CHRIST GIVEN TO THE DISCIPLES

Neither Jesus' action-packed life nor His divine mission afforded Him the occasion to commit His teachings to writings. This task was delivered to His disciples with the promise that the Holy Spirit would "bring to their remembrance" the things about Christ and "guide them into all truth."

Jesus repeatedly promised guidance in what the disciples taught.

1. Even when the twelve were first commissioned to preach "the kingdom of heaven" (Matt. 10:7), Jesus promised them, saying, "For what you are to say will be given to you in that hour; for it is not you who speak, but the Spirit of your Father speaking through you" (vv. 19-20; cf. Luke 12:11-12).

2. The same basic promise was also given to the seventy when they were authorized to preach "the kingdom of God" (Luke 10:9). Jesus said, "He who hears you hears me, and he who rejects you rejects me" (Luke 10:16).

3. Later, on the Mount of Olives, Jesus again promised His disciples, "Do not be anxious beforehand what you are to say; but say whatever is given you in that hour, for it is not you who speak, but the Holy Spirit" (Mark 13:11).

4. Still later, at the Last Supper, Jesus more clearly defined His promise to the eleven disciples, saying, "But the Counselor, the Holy Spirit, whom the Father will send in my name, he will *teach you all things*, and *bring to your remembrance* all that I have said to you" (John 14:26). He also told them, "When the Spirit of truth comes, he will *guide you into all the truth*" (John 16:13).

5. The Great Commission of Christ, given after His resurrection, contains the same promise: "And behold, I send the promise of my Father upon you" so that "repentance and forgiveness of sins should be preached in his name to all nations" (Luke 24:49, 47). In Matthew 28:18-19,

Jesus commissions the disciples with "all authority in heaven and on earth" to go and "make disciples of all nations . . . *teaching* them to observe all that I have commanded you," promising them that He would be with them always in the fulfillment of this commission to *teach* about Him (v. 20).

THE PROMISE OF CHRIST CLAIMED

Christ's promise to direct the disciples in what they taught about Him is the key to the divine authority of the New Testament, and the disciples' claim to that authority is the fulfillment of that promise. Briefly stated,

> Whatever Jesus' apostles taught originated from the Holy Spirit.
> The New Testament is what the apostles taught.
> Therefore, the New Testament originated from the Holy Spirit.

That the apostles and their associates claimed the promise of Christ in the Spirit-directed teaching of their writings is abundantly evident.

The claim to be continuing Christ's teaching. Luke's gospel, for example, claims to give an accurate account of what "Jesus *began* to do and *teach*" (Acts 1:1; cf. Luke 1:3-4). Hence, the book of Acts is giving a record of what Jesus *continued* to *teach* through the disciples. Compare with this claim the fact that the early church is characterized by devotion "to the *apostles' teaching*" (Acts 2:42), the final *authority of their pronouncements* (cf. Acts 15:22), and to the *bestowing of the Holy Spirit* through their ministry (cf. Acts 8:14-17; 10:45; 19:6).

The comparison of their writings to the Old Testament Scripture. It is further evident that the New Testament writers claimed the fulfillment of Christ's promise by placing their writings on the same level as the Old Testament Scriptures. Such is the claim made in Hebrews 1:1-2 which declares that the God who spoke by the prophets has in these last days spoken to us by His Son, which message "was declared at first by the Lord, and it was attested to us by those who heard him [viz., the apostles]" (Heb. 2:3).

Peter, in his second epistle (3:15-16), classes the writings of Paul with "the other *scriptures*," and I Timothy 5:18 refers to the gospel of Luke (10:7) under the title of "scripture."

Claim within New Testament books for their divine authority. One further confirmation that the New Testament writers felt their writings to be a fulfillment of Christ's promise comes from the claim within their books. Each book in its own way, directly or indirectly, claims to be written with divine authority.

1. The Gospels, for example, claim to be an authoritative account of the fulfillment of the Old Testament prophecies in the life of Christ (cf. Matt. 1:22; 2:15, 17, 23; 4:14, etc.). Luke wrote that Theophilus "may know the truth" about Christ (1:1, 4). John wrote that men "may believe that Jesus is the Christ, . . . and . . . have life in his name" (20:31) and adds that "his testimony is true" (21:24).

2. Acts indirectly claims to be a continuing record of that which Jesus had begun to do and *teach* in the Gospels (1:1).

3. Paul's epistles each lay claim to divine authority (cf. Rom. 1:3-5; I Cor. 14:37; II Cor. 1:1-2; Gal. 1:1, 12; Eph. 3:3; Phil. 4:9; Col. 1:1; 4:16; I Thess. 5:27; II Thess. 3:14; I Tim. 4:11; II Tim. 1:13; 4:1; Titus 2:15; Philemon 8).

4. The General Epistles also claim to be divinely authoritative. (Cf. Heb. 1:1; 2:3; James 1:1; I Peter 1:1; II Peter 3:2; I John 1:1; II John 5, 7; III John 9, 12; Jude 3; Rev. 22:9, 18-19.)

The early church confirmed this claim. Jesus promised inspiration, the New Testament writers fulfilled this promise, and the early church confirmed it. The confirmation was manifested in the fact that the New Testament books were: (1) accepted as authoritative writings (II Thess. 2:15); (2) read in the churches (I Thess. 5:27); (3) circulated among the churches; (4) quoted by other New Testament writers (cf. II Peter 3:2-3 with Jude 17-18; I Tim. 5:18 with Luke 10:7); and (5) collected along with the Old Testament Scriptures (II Peter 3:15).

Christ, then, is the key to the Bible's inspiration. What He claimed about the divine origin and binding authority of the Old Testament, He also promised for the apostolic writings of the New Testament. The evidence that this is true is seen in the fact that the inspiration which Christ promised, the writers of the New Testament claimed and the early church accepted, namely, that the New Testament writings were considered of equal divine authority with the Old Testament Scriptures.

CHRIST: THE KEY TO THE BIBLE'S CANONIZATION

The word *canon* as applied to the Bible means those writings which are considered to be the "rule" (Greek, *Kanōn*) or "norm" of faith and practice. That is, the "canon" of Scripture are those books that are constituted with divine authority. In other words, a book is "canonical" if it is inspired by God. The "canonicity" or divine authority of a book was bestowed or determined by God, who gave it that authority. Canonicity, however, had to be discovered or recognized by the men of God, who accepted and collected these writings. This raises the problem as to the earmarks or distinguishing characteristics of a canonical book. How could the church recognize which books God had inspired? The early church often looked for such earmarks as: (1) Was this book written by a man of God? (2) Does it come with the authority of God? (3) Does it tell the truth about God (as known from previous revelations)? (4) Does it have the power of God

(e. g., to edify)? (5) Was it accepted by the people of God?[1] To this list may be added another earmark which cuts across several of these (with particular application to the Old Testament), namely: Was it confirmed by the Son of God? Did Jesus refer to or quote from a book as canonical? If so, then the key to canonization can be found in the verification of Christ.

A survey has already been made of what Jesus taught about the divine authority of the Old Testament as a whole. If it can be determined which books constituted the canon of the Old Testament to which Jesus referred, then it could thereby be established what constituted the canon of which He approved. There are several lines of evidence to verify that the canon of Christ is identical with that of the Jewish and Protestant Old Testament of today.

The Jewish Old Testament of today consists of twenty-four books but is identical with the Protestant Old Testament which numbers thirty-nine books because the former "combines" the twelve Minor Prophets into one book, as it does Kings, Samuel, Chronicles, and Ezra-Nehemiah. The Jews also sometimes enumerated their books as twenty-two in number, when Ruth is combined with Judges, and Lamentations with Jeremiah, thus corresponding with the number of letters in the Hebrew alphabet. The Roman Catholic Old Testament, on the other hand, has seven more books (and four parts of books), totaling forty-six and four parts of books. These are known as Apocryphal books and consist of (1) Tobit; (2) Judith; (3) The Wisdom of Solomon; (4) Ecclesiasticus (or Sirach); (5) Baruch and Letter of Jeremiah; (6) I Maccabees; (7) II Maccabees; (8) Additions to Esther (10:4—16:24);[2] (9) The Prayer of Azariah and the Song of the Three Young Men (inserted after Dan. 3:23);

[1]For further elaboration of this point see N. L. Geisler and William Nix, A General Introduction to the Bible (Chicago: Moody, 1968), chap. 11.
[2]The Jewish and Protestant Old Testament ends at Dan. 12 and Esther 10:3.

(10) Susanna (Dan. 13); and (11) Bel and the Dragon (Dan. 14).[2]

Did Jesus consider these books to be part of the inspired canon of Scripture? The evidence is clearly against such a view for several reasons.

THE TESTIMONY OF JESUS ABOUT THE CANON

As has been already noted, the most common designations of the complete canon of the Old Testament in Jesus' day was the phrase "the Law and the Prophets." This phrase occurs about twelve times in the New Testament (cf. Matt. 5:17; Luke 16:16; Acts 24:14), and each time it is meant to include the *whole* Old Testament (all twenty-two books of the Jews or thirty-nine books of the Protestants). In Matthew 11:13 the scope of this phrase is clearly indicated; the "Law and Prophets" include all inspired writings from Moses up to John the Baptist. This of course does not define the precise contents of the Old Testament canon (this must be determined from other sources); what it does do, however, is to reveal the limits of the Old Testament canon as the Jewish "Law and Prophets." So the *whole* Old Testament was referred to under *two* classes, Law and Prophets. Jesus called these two sections "all the scriptures" (Luke 24:27). There is evidence from the Dead Sea community at Qumran that the Essenes at the time of Christ also referred to the *whole* Old Testament as Law and Prophets,[3] as did the writer of II Maccabees (cf. 15:9).

However, there was an early tendency, even before Jesus' day (cf. Prologue to Ecclesiasticus, 132 B.C.) to subdivide the Prophets into two sections thus having a threefold division, called today, Law, Prophets and Writings. Jesus Himself alludes to a threefold division (Luke 24:44), calling the Old Testament, "the law of Moses and the prophets and the psalms." Whatever the division, the contents were the same, as will become apparent shortly.

[3]Cf. *Manual of Discipline*, I, 3; VIII, 15.

THE CONTENTS OF JESUS' OLD TESTAMENT CANON

Josephus, the Jewish historian from the time of Christ (A.D. 37-100), is the best nonbiblical source for the contents of the canon to which Christ referred. Did it include the Apocryphal books or only the twenty-two books of the Hebrew Bible of today? Josephus' answer is very clear:

> For we have not an ennumerable multitude of books among us . . . but only twenty-two books . . . which are justly believed to be divine; and of them [1] five belong to Moses . . . [2] the prophets, who were after Moses, wrote down what was done in their times in thirteen books. [3] The remaining four books contain hymns to God, and precepts for the conduct of human life.[4]

The testimony of Josephus is instructive because he explicitly excludes any books written between 400 B.C. and A.D. 100 (his day). He says,

> It is true our history hath been written since Artaxerxes [424 B.C.], very particularly, but hath not been esteemed of the like authority with the former by our forefathers, because there hath not been an exact succession of prophets since that time.[5]

That is, the Jews have not considered any book to be inspired since Malachi. Now since the Apocryphal books (officially added to the Bible in A.D. 1546 by the Roman Catholic Church) were written in the period between 200 B.C. and A.D. 100, they would be explicitly excluded, as indeed they are in the list of twenty-two books Josephus gave.

Jesus' use of the Old Testament settles the question on the contents of the canon without any corroboration from contemporary Jewish sources. First, in Matthew 23:35 Jesus defined the limits of Old Testament inspired history as between the martyrs Abel (Genesis) and Zechariah (II Chron. 24:20

---

[4]Josephus, *Against Apion*, I, 8.
[5]*Ibid.*

or 36:15-16). Now since there were many Jewish martyrs in the Apocryphal books after this time (cf. II Maccabees 2, 5, 6, 7), the statement of Jesus is obviously exclusive of these as being part of inspired Old Testament history. Furthermore, in numerous quotations and references from every major section of the Old Testament from the first chapter of Genesis (1:27, cf. Matt. 19:4) to the last chapter of Malachi (4:5, cf. Mark 9:12), *Jesus never once quotes from or refers to any Apocryphal books.*[6] He never quotes from any book other than the twenty-two books of the Hebrew Old Testament, which correspond exactly with the thirty-nine books of the Protestant Old Testament.

JESUS' CITATIONS FROM THE LAW

Genesis 1:27 was quoted by Jesus in His reply to the Pharisees: "Have you not read that he who made them from the beginning made them male and female . . . ?" (Matt. 19:4-5). Exodus 16:4, 15 is quoted in John 6:31, "As it is written, 'He gave them bread from heaven to eat.'" Leviticus is referred to when Jesus told the leper to "offer the gift that Moses commanded" (Matt. 8:4, cf. Lev. 14:2). Jesus alluded to Numbers in John 3:14 when He said, "As Moses lifted up the serpent in the wilderness. . . ." (cf. Num. 21:9). Deuteronomy, of all books of the Law, was quoted most by Jesus. He resisted Satan with three quotes from Deuteronomy (Matt. 4:4, cf. Deut. 8:3; Matt. 4:7, cf. Deut. 6:16; Matt. 4:10, cf. Deut. 6:13). In Mark 12:29, Jesus cites the famous passage of Deuteronomy 6:4 when He says, "The Lord our God, the Lord is one." Deuteronomy 24:1-4, on divorce, is referred to by Jesus (Mark 10:4), as well as the kinsman law of Deuteronomy 25:5 (Matt. 22:24), and others.

[6]While it is also true that Old Testament books such as Esther and Song of Solomon were not individually verified by Christ, nevertheless they did meet the tests for canonicity. At any rate they are not the books under dispute. The burden of proof rests with those who would contest that Jesus and/or the Jews did accept the Apocrypha.

JESUS' CITATION FROM THE PROPHETS

The Prophets comprised the rest of the Old Testament. Most of these books were cited by Jesus. Joshua and Judges are not referred to by Jesus, but Samuel and Kings are. The eating of the "bread of the Presence" by David (I Sam. 21:1-6) is mentioned in Matthew 12:3-4. The ministry of Elijah to the widow (I Kings 17) is mentioned in Luke 4:25. Chronicles is referred to in Matthew 23:35 (cf. II Chron. 24:21). Ezra-Nehemiah is probably mentioned in John 6:31 (cf. Neh. 9:15), "He gave them bread from heaven to eat" (although this quote may be adapted from Ps. 78:24 or 105:40). Esther is not referred to by Jesus directly nor is Job.

Psalms, however, is one of the books most often quoted by Jesus. He quoted from Psalms (1) at the age of twelve (Luke 2:49, cf. Ps. 26:8; 27:4); (2) in the Sermon on the Mount (Matt. 5:35; 7:23, cf. Ps. 48:2; 6:8); (3) in teaching the multitude (Matt. 13:35, cf. Ps. 78:2); (4) in weeping over Jerusalem (Matt. 23:37, cf. Ps. 91:4); (5) in purifying the temple (Matt. 21:16, cf. Ps. 8:2); (6) in answering the Jews (Matt. 21:42, cf. Ps. 118:22-23); (7) at the Last Supper (Matt. 26:30, cf. Ps. 95–98); (8) on the cross (Matt. 27:46, cf. Ps. 22:1); and (9) after His resurrection (Luke 24:44). Jesus made one possible reference to Proverbs (25:6-7, cf. Luke 14:8-10) but does not clearly refer to Ecclesiastes or the Song of Solomon.

From Isaiah, Jesus made many quotations (cf. Luke 4:18 with Isa. 61:1; John 12:38 with Isa. 53:1). Jeremiah 18 and 19 are quoted (by way of Zech. 11:12-13) in Matthew 27:9, and Lamentations (3:30) is referred to in Matthew 27:30. Ezekiel is not clearly cited by Jesus, but His reference to "living water" in John 7:38 may be an allusion to Ezekiel 47:1. Daniel is clearly cited by Christ in Matthew 24:15 (cf. Dan. 9:27), when He referred to the "abomination of desolation" (ASV). The Twelve (Minor Prophets) are quoted several times (cf. Hosea 10:8 with Luke 23:30; Zech. 13:7 with Matt. 26:31; Mal. 4:5 with Matt. 17:11).

Jesus quoted from or referred to some fifteen books of the twenty-two books of the Hebrew Old Testament canon, including books from every section, and verses from scores of chapters ranging from the first chapter of Genesis to the last chapter of Malachi, but never once did Jesus quote from or refer to any Apocryphal book. In fact, since the Apocryphal books were known to the Jews of Jesus' day but were not part of the canon which they accepted (as is clear from Josephus), then it may be safely concluded that Jesus not only *omitted* the Apocryphal books from the canon of inspired Scripture but He also definitely *excluded* them. In brief, the canon of Christ, like the canon accepted by the Palestinian Jews of His day, consisting of twenty-two (twenty-four) books, is identical with the thirty-nine books of the Protestant Old Testament of today.[7]

CHRIST: THE KEY TO THE BIBLE'S AUTHENTICATION

Not only is Christ the key to the inspiration and canonization of the Bible, but He is the key to the authentication of the historical and miraculous narrations of the Old Testament. Most of the major events of the Old Testament which Bible critics dispute were verified by Christ. One is left with the option of impugning the integrity of the Christ of the Gospels or accepting the authenticity of these events.

CHRIST'S VERIFICATION OF THE HISTORICAL CHARACTER OF OLD TESTAMENT EVENTS

Jesus personally verified the historical truth of (1) Adam and Eve (Matt. 19:4); (2) Abel's murder (Matt. 23:35);

---

[7]Even the Messianic cult at Qumran possessed Apocryphal books but apparently did not esteem them of equal value with the sacred Scriptures. Millar Burrows, *More Light on the Dead Sea Scrolls* (New York: Viking, 1958), p. 178, says of the Apocrypha, "There is no reason to think that any of these works were venerated as Sacred Scripture." Scholars cite several different lines of evidence for viewing the Apocrypha as noncanonical in Qumran: (1) the absence of any commentaries on the Apocryphal books, (2) the failure to find any Apocryphal books written on the more valuable writing materials like parchment, (3) and even the failure to find any Apocryphal books written in the special (taller) script, as were the canonical books.

(3) Noah and the flood (Luke 17:27); (4) Lot and the destruction of Sodom (Luke 17:29); (5) the existence of the patriarchs Abraham, Isaac and Jacob (Luke 13:28); (6) Moses and the burning bush (Luke 20:37); (7) the wilderness wanderings of Israel (John 3:14); (8) the story of Elijah and the widow (Luke 4:25); (9) and of Naaman the Syrian leper (Luke 4:27); (10) David and the tabernacle (Matt. 12:3-4); (11) Solomon and the queen of Sheba (Matt. 12:42); (12) Jonah and Nineveh (Matt. 12:41); and (13) Daniel the prophet (Matt. 24:15).

That Jesus held these people and events to be historical is obvious from the straightforward way which He refers to them and the authority of teaching that He bases on them. For example, when Jesus affirms, "For as Jonah *was* three days and three nights in the belly of the whale, so *will* the Son of man be three days and three nights in the heart of the earth" (Matt. 12:40), He is obviously claiming both events to be historical. Jesus would hardly contend for the reality of His death and resurrection on the basis of a mythology about Jonah.

Christ's Verification of the Miraculous Character of Old Testament Events

The events of the Old Testament were not only considered to be historical but many of them were supernatural in character. In effect, Jesus' references verify the miraculous nature of:

1. the world's destruction by a flood (Luke 17:27)
2. Lot's wife being crystallized (Luke 17:32)
3. the burning bush before Moses (Luke 20:37)
4. the healing of Israel from snakebites (John 3:14)
5. the manna from heaven (John 6:49)
6. the healing of Naaman the leper (Luke 4:26)
7. the miracles of Elijah for the widow (Luke 4:25)
8. the preservation of Jonah in the whale (Matt. 12:41)

Jesus verified all of these, to say nothing of His substantiation of the existence and personality of the devil (cf. Matt. 4:1-11), innumerable demons (cf. Mark 5:1-13), His supernatural conversation with Moses and Elijah, and the scores of miracles Jesus performed in His own day. The claim of Christ is clear: the Old Testament is a historical account of God's supernatural dealings with His people.[8]

VERIFICATION OR ACCOMMODATION?

Of course one might argue that Christ never verified the inspiration, canonicity or authenticity of the Old Testament at all. They might argue, as indeed some have, that Christ was not interested in these formal, technical matters at all but rather He engaged in an "accommodation" to the accepted Jewish tradition of His day. That is, He was not affirming, for example, the historical fact that Jonah *was* in the whale, but saying, as it were, "As you *believe* that Jonah was in the whale, so I wish to *use* this accepted tradition or myth to

[8]Whether or not Christ by His authority also verified the authorship of certain Old Testament books depends on whether His references to Moses, David, Isaiah, *et al.* are to be taken merely as *identifications* of the passage He is citing or as *verification* of the person as the author of that passage. It is true that Jesus referred to both sections of Isaiah (53:1 and 6:10) as the *same* Isaiah (John 12:38, 40) and to the first five books of the Old Testament as "the book of Moses" (Mark 12:26), "the law of Moses" (Luke 24:44), and even as Moses (Luke 16:29; 24:27). He spoke also of a psalm as David's, but the question is whether He used these names merely for the *location* of the passage cited or for a *verification* of the person who wrote it (or both). There are times when Jesus is clearly referring to the book and not to the man who wrote it, as for example when He spoke of "the *book* of Moses" (Mark 12:26), or what is "written about me in the *law* of Moses" (Luke 24:44), or, "Well did Isaiah prophesy . . . as it is written" (Mark 7:6). However, there are occasions when Jesus distinguishes between the author and his book, as when He said, "For David himself says in the Book of Psalms" (Luke 20:42), or "Moses in the law . . . wrote" (John 1:45), or "David, inspired by the Spirit, calls him Lord" (Matt. 22:43, cf. v. 42). In these passages and others, Jesus seemed to go beyond the mere title of the book and give the name of its author.

The crucial question to ask about each passage is: What is it that Jesus is *teaching?* If it can be determined that Jesus is either clearly affirming or directly implying who is the author of a given book, then this is certainly to be taken as a verification of that fact. But regardless as to how this question is answered, there can be no doubt that the numerous and categorical affirmations of Christ about the authority, historicity and authenticity of the Jewish canon of Scripture manifest clearly that He was definitely teaching these truths.

illustrate to you that. . . . " According to this view, Jesus was not making *affirmations* about the historicity, authenticity, canonicity or authority of the Old Testament, but He was engaging in *accommodations* on these questions.

The tragedy of this "beautiful" theory is that it is slain by a brutal gang of facts—facts that come from the character and content of Christ's ministry. First, it should be observed, with regard to Jesus' teaching about the inspiration of the Old Testament, that any such accommodation view stands in direct contradiction to one of the central themes of Christ's ministry. For it is not a matter of here and there, occasional references to the Old Testament by Jesus, but a constant and dominant emphasis of His ministry. If the gospel record even gives the gist of what Jesus said (and there is ample evidence that it gives far more than this),[9] then we know that Jesus believed and taught the divine authority of the Old Testament Scriptures.

Furthermore, with regard to the canonization and authentication of the Old Testament by Christ, there can be no question that *Jesus was not an accommodator.* Jesus never hesitated to rebuke existing religious views that were not true, as He did to the Jews who exalted their "traditions" above "God's commandments" (Matt. 15:1-3). Six times in the Sermon on the Mount He contrasted His affirmations with false Jewish interpretations of the Old Testament, in such phrases as "you have heard that it was said . . . but I say unto you" (Matt. 5:21-22, 27-28, 31-32, 33-34, 38-39, 43-44). Jesus often told them, as in Matthew 22:29, "You are wrong, because you know neither the scriptures nor the power of God." He rebuked the great religious leader Nicodemus, saying, "Are you a teacher of Israel, and yet you do not understand this [about the new birth]?" (John 3:10). Jesus also told men when they were right about the Old Testament, as when He said to the Pharisees about the tithes, "These you ought to

[9]See F. F. Bruce, *The New Testament Documents: Are They Reliable?* (Grand Rapids: Eerdmans, 1965), which supports this point.

have done" (Matt. 23:23), or to the lawyer's answer about love being the greatest commandment, "You have answered right" (Luke 10:28). On the other hand, when they were merely wrong—either in precept or principle—Jesus did not hesitate to call them "blind guides" (Matt. 23:16) or "false prophets" (Matt. 7:15). Christ rebuked men when they were wrong, commended them when they were right, but He is never known to have accommodated Himself to their error—certainly not to any error about the sacred Scriptures.

Of course it might be contended that it was not a matter of accommodation but of *limitation* that makes it impossible to apply the authority of Christ to historical and critical matters of the Old Testament. It is sometimes held, for example, that Jesus' knowledge of these "nonspiritual" matters was limited either because He was not really God and therefore not all-knowing or because as man it was not given to Him to know of such things. The former view is not tenable in the light of Jesus' claims nor in view of the rest of Scripture, both of which clearly affirm Him to be God.[10] In favor of the view that Christ's knowledge was limited by the incarnation has been urged the fact that He claimed to be ignorant of the time of His second coming (Mark 13:32), He appeared to be ignorant as to whether the fig tree had fruit (Mark 11:13), He was said to have "increased in wisdom" (Luke 2:52), and to have "emptied himself" (Phil. 2:7) when He became man. Without entering into detailed interpretations of these diffi-

---

[10]The claims of Christ are sometimes misunderstood by modern man, but they were not so misconstrued by His contemporaries. When Jesus said to the strict monotheistic Jews of His day, "I and the Father are one" (John 10:30), they took up stones to kill Him, because, said they, "You, being a man, make yourself God" (v. 33). Likewise, when Jesus said to the paralytic, "My son, your sins are forgiven" (Mark 2:5), the scribes rightly asked, "Who can forgive sins but God alone?" (v. 7). And when Jesus said, "Truly, truly, I say to you, before Abraham was, I am" (John 8:58), no one mistook His claim to deity (cf. the "I AM" of Exodus 3:14), for again they took up stones to kill Him. For further evidence that the Scriptures in general teach the deity of Christ, cf. also Matt. 26:64-65; Heb. 1:8.

cult passages,[11] it is sufficient to answer this objection by pointing out that the Bible clearly affirms that Christ was not limited in knowledge even in His incarnation. It says that Jesus saw Nathanael under the fig tree without being in visual distance (John 1:48), that "he knew all men" and "what was in man" (John 2:24), that He knew the reputation of the woman of Samaria (John 4:18-19), that He knew in advance who would believe and who would betray Him (John 6:64), and even "all [things] that would befall him" (John 18:4), that He knew of Lazarus' death before He was told (John 11:14), that He knew of Peter's denial in advance (Matt. 26:34), and of His own death and resurrection (Mark 9:31), as well as the events connected with the fall of Jerusalem and His own second coming (cf. Matt. 24). After demonstrating His knowledge to His disciples throughout His ministry, they declared, "Now we know that you know all things" (John 16:30).[12] Despite all of this, even if some limitation were imposed on the incarnate Christ, there certainly *could not be a limitation on the truth of what He taught.* And Jesus

[11]With regard to Mark 13:32, it may be that Jesus is not necessarily disclaiming knowledge of the time of His second coming but merely that it is the Father's function to reveal it and not the Son's (cf. Acts 1:7). Whatever Christ "emptied" Himself of in Philippians 2:7, it clearly was not His deity and the attributes that are a part of it (such as omniscience), for God cannot change or cease to be God (Mal. 3:6; James 1:17). In becoming man, Christ apparently "emptied" Himself of either the manifestation of His divine glory or the independent exercise of His divine powers. That Jesus did not know if the fig tree had fruit on it could possibly be a reference to His human vision and not to any lack of divine knowledge. Otherwise, it would be very strange indeed that He knew so many other things when separated by space or time. Finally, that Jesus grew in knowledge as a child need not be denied. The question here is whether He was limited in knowledge as a mature man, and the passage in Luke 2:52 has nothing to say about this.

[12]The Scriptures do teach that Christ was subordinated to the Father. Jesus acknowledged this when He said, "The Father is greater than I" (John 14:28) and "I have come down from heaven, not to do my own will, but the will of him who sent me" (John 6:38). The Apostle Paul taught the same when he wrote, "The head of Christ is God" (I Cor. 11:3), and, "Then shall the Son also himself be subject unto him that put all things under him, that God may be all in all" (I Cor. 15:28, AV). However, the *subordination* of the Son in His office and function in no way necessitates a *limitation* in His knowledge and nature. The Son is subordinate in *office,* but He is equivalent in *nature* with the Father (John 10:30; 5:23; 1:1). The subordination of the Son teaches only that there is order in the Godhead not that there is any limitation or error in Christ's teaching.

clearly taught the authority and authenticity of the Scriptures. Then too, it is one thing to claim that there were some human *limitations* on Jesus' human knowledge and quite another to say that He *erred* in what He taught. Just as the incarnation placed some finite limitations on Christ's infinite deity and yet He *never sinned* (Heb. 4:15; I John 3:5), likewise whatever limitations might possibly be entailed in His knowledge, it must be affirmed that He *never erred* in anything He taught (cf. John 8:40, 46). In brief, there is no evidence of any limitation on the truth of what Christ taught, and there is certainly no *error* in His teaching.

Still it may be contended that Jesus was not concerned about historical and critical matters but only theological or spiritual matters. But such is not the case, for His affirmations were about the history and authenticity of the Old Testament, and the authority of Jesus' moral and spiritual proclamations often rested on the veracity of the Old Testament people and events to which He referred (John 8:56-58). Jesus spoke to this objection when He said, "If I have told you *earthly things* and you do not believe, how can you believe if I tell you heavenly things?" (John 3:12). That is, if we cannot trust the statements of Christ about straightforward historical matters, which can be tested,[13] how can we believe what He says about spiritual matters, which cannot be so tested? The alternatives are clear enough: either Jesus was a liar, a lunatic, or Lord.[14] If He was Lord, then He is the key to the inspiration, canonization and authentication of the Old Testament. If Jesus is not Lord, then there are the other two choices, neither of which fit with the known character and

[13]For example, it can be determined by archaeological artifacts and from written documents whether or not the places and even events of the Old Testament really were or not. And, incidentally, over 25,000 sites from the biblical world have been confirmed by some archaeological discoveries to date. See D. J. Wiseman, "Archaeological Confirmation of the Old Testament" in *Revelation and the Bible,* Carl F. Henry, ed. (Grand Rapids: Baker, 1958), pp. 301-2.

[14]See Vernon Grounds, *The Reason for Our Hope* (Chicago: Moody, 1945), pp. 30-35.

influence of Christ. One thing is definite, Jesus cannot be considered a great and good moral Teacher if He was knowingly perpetrating falsehoods about the Bible. On the other hand, if Jesus was a good and great moral Teacher, then the inspiration, etc., of the Old Testament is a fact, for He said it was.

CHRIST: THE KEY TO THE BIBLE'S INTERPRETATION

Even among those who grant that Christ is the key to the aforementioned areas, it seems to be a neglected truth that Jesus is also the *key to the interpretation of the Bible.* Christ, on at least five occasions, advanced the claim that He was the theme of the entire scope of Old Testament Scriptures, and yet they are often studied with little more than scant allusions to certain prophetic and typological references about the person and work of the Saviour. The ensuing pages of this book will be an attempt to amplify and illustrate exactly how Christ may be viewed as the interpretive key that unlocks the meaning of the Bible.

2

CHRIST IN THE OLD TESTAMENT

Viewing the Old Testament Christocentrically is not an interpretive (hermeneutical) option; for the Christian it is a divine imperative. On five different occasions Jesus claimed to be the theme of the entire Old Testament: (1) Matthew 5:17; (2) Luke 24:27; (3) Luke 24:44; (4) John 5:39; (5) Hebrews 10:7.

An examination of these passages reveals that there are at least four different Christocentric ways to view the Old Testament. Each passage stresses a different sense in which Christ is the fulfillment of the Old Testament. And in each case the book in which the statement of Jesus occurs is an illustration of that particular Christocentric approach to the Old Testament. The passages read as follows:

> And beginning with Moses and all the prophets, he interpreted to them in all the scriptures the things concerning himself (Luke 24:27).
>
> Then he said to them, "These are my words which I spoke to you, while I was still with you, that everything written about me in the law of Moses and the prophets and the psalms must be fulfilled" (Luke 24:44).
>
> Then I said, "Lo, I have come to do thy will, O God," as it is written of me in the roll of the book (Heb. 10:7).[1]

[1]Although the immediate reference here is probably to the book of Psalms (40:8), from which the quote is taken, and not to the Old Testament as a whole, the fact that the Messiah is said to have undertaken to perform whatever the will of God prescribes justifies the extension of this reference to the Old Testament as a whole, insofar as it defines the will of God for Christ's priestly obedience. That this approach is justified is illustrated by the Christocentric procedure of the book of Hebrews itself (discussed below).

Think not that I have come to abolish the law and the prophets; I have come not to abolish them but to fulfil them (Matt. 5:17).

You search the scriptures, because you think that in them you have eternal life; and it is they that bear witness to me (John 5:39).

FOUR CHRISTOCENTRIC VIEWS OF THE OLD TESTAMENT

Passage	Approach: Christ Viewed as Fulfilling Old Testament	Where Illustrated	Christ Viewed as
Luke 24:27, 44	Messianic Prophecy	Luke and Acts	Messiah and King
Heb. 10:7	Levitical Priesthood	Hebrews	Priest and Sacrifice
Matt. 5:17	Moral Precepts	Matthew	Prophet and Teacher
John 5:39	Salvation Promises	John and Revelation	Saviour and Lord

CHRIST: THE FULFILLMENT OF OLD TESTAMENT
MESSIANIC PROPHECY

That the Old Testament prophets made predictions about the coming of the Christ or Messiah may be understood from many Old Testament verses themselves, without recourse to the New Testament fulfillment of them.[*] The Old Testament believers looked for the coming of a Saviour from the very beginning (cf. Gen. 3:15; 49:10), even though the word *Messiah* [anointed one] was first used of their coming King in I Samuel 2:10. Hence, a study of the Old Testament to find its *Messianic predictions* is a very legitimate and profitable, Christocentric approach. Among the inspired writings of the New Testament it seems to be Luke who gives the best illustration of how such a study may proceed.

*See page 63.

It was Luke who recorded that Jesus twice affirmed the legitimacy of this approach (Luke 24:27, 44). First, to the two disciples on the road to Emmaus, Jesus said," 'O foolish men, and slow of heart to believe all that the prophets have spoken! Was it not necessary that the Christ should suffer these things and enter into his glory?' And beginning with Moses and all the prophets, *he interpreted to them in all the scriptures the things concerning himself*" (24:26-27). With the fresh impression of this divine exposition of Old Testament Messianic Scriptures yet burning within their hearts, they reported their experience to the eleven (24:32-35). Before their report was finished, Jesus appeared to the group, and, having eaten with them, He said, "These are my words which I spoke to you, while I was still with you, that *everything written about me* in the law of Moses and the prophets and the psalms *must be fulfilled*" (24:44).

It has often been wondered just what Jesus told these disciples and exactly what was the content of His own Christocentric approach to the Old Testament. But one need not wonder, for Luke amply illustrates the approach in his gospel and Acts. The general approach, however, was given first by Christ Himself to the disciples when "he opened their minds to understand the scriptures, and said to them, 'Thus it is written, that the Christ should suffer and on the third day rise from the dead, and that repentance and forgiveness of sins should be preached in his name to all nations . . . .' " (24:45-47). This is to say, that Christ pointed them to the great *Messianic predictions* of the Old Testament about His own death, resurrection, and the consequent world evangelization.

MESSIANIC PREDICTIONS QUOTED IN LUKE'S GOSPEL

It is in the book of Acts that Luke best illustrates Christ's approach to Messianic prophecy, but even in his gospel there are many passages. Luke points to the fact that the Old Testament predicted:

1. the ministry of the Messiah's forerunner (Luke 1:17, cf. Mal. 4:5-6)
2. the mention of His birthplace (Luke 2:11, cf. Micah 5:2)
3. the introduction by John the Baptist (Luke 3:4-6, cf. Isa. 40:3-5; Luke 7:27, cf. Mal. 3:1)
4. Christ's claim in the synagogue at Nazareth (Luke 4:18-19, cf. Isa. 61:2)
5. the triumphal entry (Luke 19:38, cf. Ps. 118:26)
6. the cleansing of the temple (Luke 19:46; Isa. 56:7; Jer. 7:11)
7. the rejected cornerstone (Luke 20:17, cf. Ps. 118:22)
8. David's Lord (Luke 20:42, cf. Ps. 110:1)
9. Son of Man returning in glory (Luke 21:27; Dan. 7:13)
10. Christ being numbered with the transgressors (Luke 22:37; Isa. 53:12)
11. casting lots for His garments (Luke 23:34, cf. Ps. 22:18)

Most of these verses in Luke's gospel refer to the *life* and *ministry* of the Messiah. In the book of Acts, Luke records the use of many more Messianic predictions, most of which refer to the *death* and *resurrection* of Christ and the ministry of the gospel to the Gentiles, undoubtedly illustrating what Jesus Himself had taught the disciples from the Old Testament after His resurrection (Luke 24:46-47). In other words, Luke appears to be illustrating from apostolic preaching in the book of Acts the very Christocentric approach that Jesus taught the disciples in His postresurrection appearance.

MESSIANIC PREDICTIONS IN THE BOOK OF ACTS

The Acts of the Apostles records the *Messianic predictions* and fulfillments about:

1. the pouring out of the Holy Spirit (Acts 2:17-21, from Joel 2:28-32)
2. the bodily resurrection of Christ (Acts 2:25-28 [cf. 13:35], from Ps. 16:8-11)

3. David's Lord (Acts 2:34-35, from Ps. 110:1)
4. Prophet like unto Moses (Acts 3:22-23 [cf. 7:37], from Deut. 18:15, 19)
5. blessing of Abraham's seed (Acts 3:25, from Gen. 22:18)
6. rejected cornerstone (Acts 4:11, from Ps. 118:22)
7. royal rejection of the Messiah (Acts 4:25-26, from Ps. 2:1-2)
8. the sheep led to slaughter (Acts 8:32-33, from Isa. 53:7-8)
9. the Son begotten from the dead (Acts 13:33, from Ps. 2:7)
10. the sure blessings of David (Acts 13:34, from Isa. 55:3)
11. the Light for the Gentiles (Acts 13:47, from Isa. 49:6)
12. the tabernacle of David (Acts 15:16, from Amos 9:11)
13. Gentile salvation (Acts 15:17-18, from Amos 9:12)
14. Messianic blindness of the Jews (Acts 28:26-27, from Isa. 6:9-10).

So, then, Jesus *explained* that the Old Testament contained Messianic predictions about Himself, and the apostles *illustrated* what Jesus meant by this, particularly in the book of Acts. Further elaboration of this approach is evident in Romans and Galatians, where Paul, with whom Luke was associated, applies even more Old Testament passages to Christ.[2]

[2]Of the Messianic predictions not mentioned in Acts, these may be added from Romans and Galatians. They prophecy about:
1. the descent and resurrection of Christ (Rom. 10:6-7, from Deut. 30:12, 14)
2. unashamed believers (Rom. 10:11, from Isa. 28:16)
3. blessings of gospel preachers (Rom. 10:15, from Isa. 52:7)
4. global proclamation of the gospel (Rom. 10:18, cf. Ps. 19:4)
5. provoking the Jews to jealousy (Rom. 10:19, cf. Deut. 32:21)
6. disobedient Israel (Rom. 10:20-21, from Isa. 65:1-2)
7. blindness of Israel (Rom. 11:8-10, from Ps. 69:22-23)
8. Deliverer from Zion (Rom. 11:26, from Isa. 59:20-21)
9. covenant of forgiveness (Rom. 11:27, from Isa. 27:9)
10. confessing the Lord (Rom. 14:11, from Isa. 45:23)
11. salvation of Gentiles (Rom. 15:9-12, 21, from Ps. 18:49; Deut. 32:43; Ps. 117:1; Isa. 11:10; 52:15)
12. blessing of Abraham (Gal. 3:8, from Gen. 12:3)
13. curse of the cross (Gal. 3:13, from Deut. 21:23)
14. Seed of Abraham (Gal. 3:16, from Gen. 13:15; 17:8)

These lists do not exhaust the Messianic prophecies of the Old Testament; they merely suggest some of the main passages applied to the life, death, resurrection and propagation of the Messiah. They, in fact, illustrate the approach to the Old Testament taken by Christ when He appeared to His disciples after the resurrection.

CHRIST: THE FULFILLMENT OF THE OLD TESTAMENT LEVITICAL PRIESTHOOD

The Messianic sense is by no means the only sense in which Christ is the theme and fulfillment of the Old Testament. Another Christocentric view of the Old Testament was suggested by Jesus' quote in Hebrews 10:5-7 (from Ps. 40:6-8). In this passage the emphasis is not upon the coming of the Messiah or anointed King but upon the perfect Priest, not upon the One who fulfills the Jewish expectation of a Ruler but of One who makes provision for them as a Mediator. The complete quote reads as follows: "Consequently, when Christ came into the world, he said, 'Sacrifices and offerings thou hast not desired, but a body hast thou prepared for me; in burnt offerings and sin offerings thou hast taken no pleasure. Then I said, "Lo, I have come to do thy will, O God," as it is written of me in the roll of the book.' " It is evident from the immediate context here, as well as from the whole of the book of Hebrews, that Christ is *written in the roll of the book* of the Old Testament in the sense that He fulfills the *Levitical priesthood* and sacrificial system.

It is true that the book of Hebrews adds many more verses to the repertoire of Messianic prophecy as:

1. "Thy throne, O God, is forever and ever" (1:8, from Ps. 45:6)
2. "Thou hast loved righteousness" (1:9, from Ps. 45:7)
3. "Thy God, has anointed thee" (1:9, from Ps. 45:7)
4. "Thou, Lord, didst found the earth" (1:10-11, from Ps. 102:25-26)

5. "What is man that thou art mindful of him" (2:6-8, from Ps. 8:4-6)
6. "I will proclaim thy name to my brethren" (2:12, from Ps. 22:22)
7. "I will put my trust in him" (2:13, from Isa. 8:17-18).

THE FULFILLMENT OF THE AARONIC PRIESTHOOD

The main emphasis, however, in Hebrews is on Christ's fulfillment of the Aaronic priesthood, as is illustrated in the following discussion.

CHRIST PERFECTS THE PATTERN OF THE OLD TESTAMENT PRIESTHOOD

A comparison of the priesthood of Aaron and that of Christ will readily reveal that they both follow the same pattern. For what was prefigured in the pattern of Aaron was perfected in the priesthood of Christ.

The Pattern	Its Perfection
What Aaron Did:	What Christ Did:
Entered the Earthly Tabernacle	Entered the Heavenly Temple (6:19)
Entered Once a Year	Entered Once for All (9:25-26)
Entered Beyond the Veil	Rent the Veil (10:20)
Offered Many Sacrifices	Offered One Sacrifice (10:11-12)
Offered for His Own Sin	Offered Only for Our Sin (7:27)
Offered Blood of Bulls	Offered His Own Blood (9:12)

CHRIST ESTABLISHES A NEW ORDER OF PRIESTHOOD

The Levitical priesthood was imperfect; therefore, it

looked to that which was perfect. There are at least seven ways in which the Levitical order was transcended by Christ. For although He was a Priest after the *pattern* of Aaron (see accompanying chart), Christ was a Priest after the *order* of Melchizedek, an order which was far superior to the order of Aaron. This new order superseded the Levitical priesthood in the following ways:

The Nature of:	The Order of Aaron: Levitical Priesthood	The Order of Melchizedek: Christ's Priesthood
consecration	temporal	eternal (7:21-23)
priest	fallible	sinless (7:26)
priesthood	changeable	unchangeable (7:24)
ministry	continual	final (9:12, 26)
mediation	imperfect	perfect (2:14-18)
sacrifice	insufficient (to take away sin)	all-sufficient (10:11-12)
intercession	not all-prevailing	all-prevailing (7:25)

The Levitical order was imperfect and temporal and so it prefigured one that would be perfect and eternal. The old order was but a shadow of the substance to be found in Christ's priestly work; it provided the ritual and ceremony, and Christ supplied the reality and efficacy.

CHRIST FULFILLS THE TYPES OF THE TABERNACLE

Not only was the priesthood of the Old Testament a prefiguration of Christ, but the tabernacle and offerings were also types of Christ. Moses was told to construct the tabernacle after the pattern revealed to him on the mount, because it served as "a copy and shadow of the heavenly sanctuary" (Heb. 8:5). The application of the tabernacle is not given in detail (cf. 9:5) by the writer of Hebrews, but the New

Testament does not leave one confused as to how this may be done.

John tells us that "The Word [Christ] became flesh and dwelt [tabernacled or pitched His tent] among us" and "we . . . beheld his glory" (John 1:14). Hebrews informs us that Jesus opened a new and living way for the believer "through the curtain, that is, through his flesh" (10:20). On this basis, it has been customary among Christians to make an identification between the function of the tabernacle's furniture and the person of Christ. Such a study might easily be pushed to fanciful extremes, but one would seem to be within safe limits if the correlation is kept within the confines of what Christ and the New Testament claim for Him. (See accompanying chart.)

CHRIST FULFILLS THE TABERNACLE TYPES

Tabernacle Type	Christ's Claim
The One Door	I Am the Door (John 10:9)
Brazen Altar	A Ransom for Many (Mark 10:45)
Laver	If I Do Not Wash You (John 13:8, 10)
Lamps	I Am the Light (John 8:12)
Bread	I Am the Bread (John 6:48)
Incense	I Am Praying for Them (John 17:9)
Veil	This Is My Body (Matt. 26:26)
Mercy Seat	I Lay Down My Life for the Sheep (John 10:15)

In the Old Testament, the tabernacle was the place that gave (1) identification to God's presence, which in the New Testament becomes (2) the incarnation of God's person (John 1:14), and both the type and its fulfillment give (3) an illustration of God's plan of salvation, which involves:

1. one approach—through the gate
2. by substitution—at the brazen altar
3. then, purification—in the laver
4. with illumination—from the lamps
5. and sustenance—from the bread
6. all by representation—of the priest
7. with intercession—at the altar of incense
8. involving expiation by blood—on the mercy seat

The various kinds of offerings likewise prefigure the all-sufficiency of Christ's sacrifice. There were five basic offerings in the Levitical system: (1) burnt; (2) meal (cereal); (3) peace; (4) sin; (5) trespass (guilt). The first three (known as sweet-savor offerings) were offerings of *dedication* and the last two (known as nonsweet-savor offerings) were offerings of *expiation*. In other words, the first three were offerings of *acceptance* (to God) and the last two, offerings of *atonement* (for man). Now the life and sufferings of Christ were acceptable to God (fulfilling the burnt, meal and peace offerings), and His death on the cross made an atonement and provision for sin (fulfilling the sin and trespass offerings). (See Matt. 3:17; Isa. 53:10-11.)

CHRIST FULFILLS THE LEVITICAL OFFERINGS

The Offering:	Fulfilled in Christ's:
Burnt Offering	Perfection of Life (Heb. 9:14)
Meal Offering	Presentation of Life (Heb. 5:7; John 4:34) or Dedication
Peace Offering	Peace for Our Life (Heb. 4:1 ff.; Eph. 2:14)
Sin Offering	Penalty for Offense (Heb. 10:12; I John 2:2)
Trespass Offering	Provision for Offender (Heb. 10:20 ff.; I John 1:7)

The Fulfillment of the Festal System

Not only does Christ fulfill the Levitical ceremonies of the Old Testament but also the festal ceremonies. The festive holidays were national in their intention and prophetic in their implications. There are seven significant annual feasts mentioned in Leviticus 23.

CHRIST FULFILLS THE LEVITICAL FEASTS

The Feast (Lev. 23):	The Fulfillment:
Passover (April)	Death of Christ (I Cor. 5:7)
Unleavened Bread (April)	Holy Walk for Christ (I Cor. 5:8)
First Fruits (April)	Resurrection of Christ (I Cor. 15:23)
Pentecost (June)	Outpouring of Spirit of Christ (Acts 1:5; 2:4)
Trumpets (Sept.)	Israel's Regathering by Christ (Matt. 24:31)
Atonement (Sept.)	Cleansing by Christ (Rom. 11:26)
Tabernacles (Sept.)	Rest and Reunion with Christ (Zech 14:16-18)

This Christocentric interpretation of the feasts goes beyond the book of Hebrews but, it would seem, not beyond the New Testament limitations of what was apparently meant in Hebrews 10:5-7, when it asserted that *Christ is the fulfillment of the Old Testament Levitical and ceremonial system.*

Christ: The Fulfillment of the Old Testament Moral Precepts

There is still another sense in which the whole Old Testament is about Christ, and this is indicated in Matthew 5:17, where Jesus is apparently claiming to be the fulfillment of the Old Testament *moral precepts.* "Think not that I have come to abolish the law and the prophets;" said Jesus, "I have not come to abolish them but *to fulfil them.*" The sense in which Christ is the fulfillment of the Old Testament is not merely that in which the Old Testament made direct *predictions* about Christ, as was often the case in Messianic prophecy. Nor is He the fulfillment of the Old Testament in the sense that He portrayed what was *prefigured* in the ceremonial system. The sense of this Christocentric interpretation includes the fact that He *perfects,* fills up, or fulfills, the *Old Testament moral precepts.*

It is important to observe the context in which this affirmation of Jesus is made. It is amid the great moral precepts of the Sermon on the Mount. Jesus has just stated the great moral Beatitudes (Matt. 5:1-11) and is just about to give the inward, spiritual sense in which the Old Testament should be understood (5:21-48). But just before Jesus gives these great moral declarations about the Old Testament, He reminds the people that He has not come to abolish but to fulfill the Old Testament. It seems obvious enough that He means that His life and teaching will bring to fruition and perfection the moral teachings which the Old Testament *pronounced* but the people could not *perform.* Jesus is here announcing that what the Old Testament prescribed morally is exactly what He will perfect and fulfill.

Later, the Apostle Paul saw this truth and wrote, "For God has done what the law, weakened by the flesh, could not do: sending his own Son in the likeness of sinful flesh and for sin, he condemned sin in the flesh, in order that the just requirement of the law might be fulfilled in us, who walk not according to the flesh but according to the Spirit" (Rom. 8:3-4). That is, the principles of the moral law, which were a reflection of the unchangeable character of God and which were embodied in and demanded by the Mosaic moral law, were perfectly fulfilled by Christ, and therefore by grace can be administered to the believer.

Jesus declared at His baptism that it was His desire to "*fulfil* all righteousness" (Matt. 3:15), and then in His great sermon He proclaims His intent to "*fulfil*" the Law and the Prophets. Both declarations contain one and the same sense in which Christ is the sum of the Old Testament Scriptures, namely, He is the fulfillment or perfection of their *moral precepts.*

Two key words in Matthew's Christocentric interpretation to the Old Testament are *righteousness* (or *righteous*) and *fulfill. Righteousness* or *righteous,* for example, are used about twenty-five times in Matthew's gospel.[3] He speaks of Joseph as righteous (or just, 1:19); of the sunshine and rain on the righteous (5:45); of Christ not calling the (self) righteous to repent (9:13); of receiving a righteous man and a righteous man's reward (three times, 10:41); of righteous men (13:17, 43, 48); of righteous dealings (20:4, 7); of outward, apparent righteousness (23:28); of the graves of the righteous (23:29); of the blood of the righteous (two times, 23:35); of the righteous at His return (25:37, 46); of Christ Himself (27:19, 24). Righteousness is referred to as (1) what Christ came to fulfill (3:15); (2) what some hungered for (5:6); (3) that for which some were persecuted (5:10); (4) that in which the Pharisees must be exceeded (5:20); (5) what one should seek (6:33); (6) a way of life (21:32). From the foregoing passages it is easy to see that Jesus was calling men from their own self-righteous way to seek God's righteousness, which He had come to fulfill.

It is this word *fulfill* that needs some clarification. It is sometimes mistakenly thought that it always means the coming to pass of a prediction, but a study of its usage in the New Testament, and particularly in Matthew, does not bear out this supposed meaning in all cases. Fulfill may mean simply (1) to fill or fill up (cf. John 15:11; Luke 2:40); or (2) to complete, consummate (cf. John 7:8, 30); or (3) realize, effectuate (cf. Gal. 5:14; Rom. 13:8). The third meaning seems to be the significance of Christ's claim to fulfill (i. e.,

---

[3]In contrast, *righteous* and *righteousness* are only used nineteen times in the other three Gospels combined.

to realize, effectuate) the Old Testament. That is, the Old Testament moral precepts are realized in and effectuated by the life and teaching of Christ.

ILLUSTRATION FROM OLD TESTAMENT QUOTATIONS

It is significant to note in this regard that there are definite passages in Matthew in which the word fulfill *does not mean the coming to pass of what was previously forecast*. Fulfill is used fifteen times of Christ in Matthew (1:22; 2:15, 17, 23; 3:15; 4:14; 5:17; 8:17; 12:17; 13:35; 21:4; 26:54, 56; 27:9, 35). Of these passages, several clearly substantiate the thesis that the Old Testament passages applied to Christ were not all truly predictive, but there was a principle in the passages which was realized or perfected in Christ.

A reading of Hosea 11:1 *in context* yields the meaning that God's calling "His son out of Egypt" refers to the nation's deliverance at the time of the exodus from Egypt (Exodus 4:22). And yet this passage is applied to the return of the Christ Child from Egypt with these words: "That it might be *fulfilled*" (Matt. 2:15, AV). It seems obvious enough that Hosea 11:1 did not directly predict the return of Jesus from Egypt, and yet this event is referred to as a fulfillment of that Old Testament verse. It is indeed a fulfillment of what Hosea said if *fulfill* means to realize the basic principle involved in that passage, namely, the Messianic mission of Israel. For, the reason God called them out of Egypt and into the holy land was for the purpose of producing the holy Child Jesus, who would save them from their sins (cf. Gen. 12:1 with Matt. 1:21). In this sense the Messianic nation only fulfills itself in effecting the Messianic mission, which was to produce the Messiah. Hosea did not here foretell of Christ, but Christ did fulfill what Hosea said in that He effectuated and realized in His life, in a more perfect way, what is meant by "my son" and "called out of Egypt."

It may be objected that in this broad sense of the word *fulfill* almost anything in the Old Testament could be applied to Christ. Indeed, it would appear that this is precisely the case. In fact, this illustrates perfectly what is implied in Jesus' assertion that the *whole Old Testament* is "fulfilled" in Him (Matt. 5:17). One would hardly suspect, for example, that Jeremiah 31:15 meant anything more than Rachel's lament for the Babylonian captivity of her children, but Matthew says this is "fulfilled" in the slaughter of the innocent children by Herod (Matt. 2:18). Nor, would one be able to guess from Isaiah 11:1 *alone* that, when referring to Christ as "branch" (*Nezer*), that this was a prediction of the fact He would live in Nazareth ("the city of shrubs").[4] Likewise, it is not evident from Psalm 78:2 that Asaph is speaking of Christ's parabolic method of teaching when he wrote, as Matthew quotes him, "I will open my mouth in parables, I will utter what has been hidden since the foundation of the world" (Matt. 13:35), nor that Zechariah (Zech. 11:12-13, cf. Jer. 32:6, 8) meant to predict the amount of the betrayal money when he referred to his wages from the sheep traders (Matt. 26:15). But in all these cases there is a *principle* involved, whether a Messianic or moral one, that is realized or comes to the full in the life of Christ. It is in this broad sense of the word *fulfill* that Jesus refers to Himself as the fulfillment of Old Testament righteousness in Matthew 5:17.

Christ was "born under the law" (Gal. 4:4), explicated its true and inner meaning in His teaching, and exemplified its principles perfectly in His life. Jesus pointed out that the essence of the law is love (Matt. 5:43, cf. 22:37-40), and love was what He performed most perfectly (cf. John 15:13). What the law demanded, only Christ supplied; therefore, the whole Old Testament was a *preparation* of the perfection and fulfillment that Christ manifested in His life.

CHRIST'S TEACHING IS THE FULFILLMENT OF THE
OLD TESTAMENT

Most of what has been said so far applies to the *life* of Christ

[4]See Lange's *Commentary on the Holy Scriptures* (Grand Rapids: Zondervan, n.d.) on Matt. 2:23 for an elaboration of this point.

as the fulfillment or perfection of the Old Testament moral precepts. However, the *teachings* of Christ should be included in what is meant by His coming to fulfill the Old Testament. Perhaps this point is best seen from the immediate context of Matthew 5:17, where Jesus contrasts His interpretation of the Old Testament with the distorted tradition of His day. "You have heard that it was said to the men of old. . . . But I say to you" (5:21-22, 27-28, 21-32, 33-34, 38-39, 43-44), Jesus repeated six times. In each of these great affirmations Christ sets off the *spirit* of the law (which He affirmed) from the *letter* of the law (which the Jews taught). His teaching went to the heart of the Old Testament and brought out the heart of the Old Testament. The Pharisees, in contrast, had either obscured or destroyed the true meaning of the Scriptures. It should be noticed that Jesus refers to their misinterpretation by the phrase "you have heard" and not "it is written." When Christ says, "But I say to you," He is reaffirming the true meaning of the Old Testament. Or better yet, Christ is "bringing out" or "filling up" the true meaning which the Old Testament contained.

They had "heard" that the *act* of murder was wrong, but Jesus taught what was really implied in what was "written," namely, that even the *thought* of murder (hatred) was wrong (Matt. 5:21-22). Again, they had "heard" that the *act* of adultery was wrong, but Jesus shows that the true implication of this command meant that even *lustful intents* are wrong. And in the last passage, part of what was "said" of old is not even in the Old Testament, let alone being misinterpreted. "You shall love your neighbor" is there to be sure, but "and hate your enemy" is not (5:43). Rather, "Love your enemies" is definitely implied in the Old Testament (cf. Prov. 24:17). It is the explication of these latent teachings of the Old Testament that are fulfilled or "brought to the full" in the teachings of Christ.

47

CHRIST: THE FULFILLMENT OF SALVATION PROMISES

There is one more passage, John 5:39-40, in which Christ claims to be the message of the whole Old Testament. He said to the Jews, "You [do] search the scriptures, because you think that in them [not, through them] you have eternal life; and [yet] it is they [the Scriptures] that bear witness to me; yet you refuse to come to me that you may have life [which you are supposedly searching for].[5] The explicit meaning of this passage must be supplied from the context. It was a warning against searching for eternal life *in* the Scriptures, as an end in themselves, rather than finding eternal life in Christ *through* the Scriptures. Such bibliolatry (worship of the Bible) really led them away from Christ rather than leading them to Christ. They knew the shell of the Bible but were neglecting the kernel within it. It is not the Book that saves, but the Saviour of the Book. This is a kind of fourth way in which Christ may be seen in the Old Testament, namely, as *the fulfillment of its salvation promises.* This is somewhat different from the other three Christocentric approaches. (1) The Messianic predictions portray Christ as Messiah and King; (2) the Levitical system reveals Him as Priest and Sacrifice, and (3) the moral precepts as the great Prophet and Teacher; but (4) Christ as the fulfillment of the Old Testament spiritual promises pictures Him as the Saviour and Lord. To the degree that the Old Testament offers the hope of salvation and eternal life, to that degree it speaks of Christ. Further, the degree to which the Old Testament speaks of Christ, to that degree it thereby offers eternal life.

The gospel of John itself is an illustration of this Christocentric approach to the Old Testament. Christ is the Life-giver and Saviour throughout the Old Testament Scriptures. Now such a claim is tantamount to identifying Himself with God, for in the Old Testament it is only God that saves. "I

[5] J. B. Phillips translates this, "You pore over the scriptures, for you imagine that you will find eternal life in them. And all the time they give their testimony to me! But you are not willing to come to me to have real life!"

am the Lord, and besides me there is no savior" (Isa. 43:11).
But John writes of Christ, "This is indeed the Savior of the
world" (John 4:42).

Now such a Christocentric interpretation of the Jewish
Scriptures, which applies all the salvation passages to Christ,
would be expected to arouse some monotheistic animosity,
which is exactly what it did. Jesus said, "I and the Father are
one." Then "the Jews took up stones again to stone him,"
which they said they were doing "for blasphemy; because you,
being a man, make yourself God" (John 10:30-31, 33). On
a previous occasion, Jesus had called God His "Father," and
"this was why the Jews sought all the more to kill him, because he . . . called God his Father, making himself equal
with God" (John 5:18).

There was no question in the Jews' mind as to what Jesus
meant by His claims. When He said, "Truly, truly, I say to
you, before Abraham was, *I am*," they again "took up stones

JESUS IS JEHOVAH

Of Jehovah	Mutual Title or Act	Of Jesus
Isa. 40:28	Creator	John 1:3
Isa. 45:22; 43:11	Saviour	John 4:42
I Sam. 2:6	Raise dead	John 5:21
Joel 3:12	Judge	John 5:27, cf. Matt. 25:31 ff.
Isa. 60:19-20	Light	John 8:12
Exodus 3:14	I Am	John 8:58, cf. 18:5-6
Ps. 23:1	Shepherd	John 10:11
Isa. 42:8, cf. 48:11	Glory of God	John 17:1, 5
Isa. 41:4; 44:6	First and Last	Rev. 1:17; 2:8
Hosea 13:14	Redeemer	Rev. 5:9
Isa. 62:5 (and Hosea 2:16)	Bridegroom	Rev. 21:2, cf. Matt. 25:1 ff.

to throw at him" (John 8:58-59). They understood Him to lay claim to deity, that is, to be the great "I *AM*" of Exodus 3:14. The same may be said of Jesus' other claims. Compare, for example, John 12:41, where John, after quoting Isaiah 6 about the glory of God, says: "Isaiah said this because he saw his [Jesus'] glory and spoke of him." The accompanying chart illustrates abundantly that the *Jesus of the New Testament is the Jehovah of the Old Testament.*

In all of these passages Jesus is either claiming (or acclaimed) to be exactly what is reserved only for Jehovah in the Old Testament. Take, for example, Isaiah 45:22: "Turn to me and be saved, all the ends of the earth! For I am God, and there is no other," and yet Jesus is the One who *saves* and forgives sins: "For you will die in your sins unless you believe that I am he," Jesus said (John 8:24). Isaiah 42:8 is even stronger: "I am the LORD, that is my name; my glory I give to no other." And yet Jesus *shared* in this glory even before the world was (John 17:5), and John says that it was *Jesus'* glory (John 12:41) of which Isaiah spoke.

Although this kind of Christocentric approach to the Old Testament is characteristic of John and Revelation, it is not exclusive to these books. In the accompanying chart are some additional selected texts showing that Jesus is Jehovah, that is, the God of the Old Testament.

The last reference is a very strong declaration of Christ's

Jehovah (God)	Mutual Title or Act	Jesus
Ps. 18:2	Rock	I Cor. 10:4
Jer. 31:34	Forgiver of Sins	Mark 2:7, 10
Ps. 148:2	Worshiped by Angels	Heb. 1:6
Throughout O.T.	Addressed in Prayer	Acts 7:59
Ps. 148:5	Creator of Angels	Col. 1:16
Isa. 45:23	Confessed as Lord	Phil. 2:10

deity. In Isaiah 45, Jehovah speaks, saying, "For I am God, and there is no other. By myself I have sworn, . . . 'To me every knee shall bow, every tongue shall swear' " (Isa. 45:22-23). These very words are applied to Christ: "That at the name of Jesus every knee should bow . . . and every tongue confess that Jesus Christ is Lord [*Jehovah,* from Isaiah], to the glory of God the Father" (Phil. 2:10). Jesus is Jehovah, and some day everyone will confess it.

In line with viewing the Lord and Saviour of the Old Testament to be Jesus, as John 5:39 would seem to suggest, is the identification of the "angel of the LORD (Jehovah)" with Jesus.

ANGEL OF THE LORD IS THE LORD JESUS CHRIST

Reference to the Angel of the Lord	Common Activity or Attribute	Reference to Christ
Gen. 16:7, 13	Called "Lord"	John 20:28
Gen. 48:15-16	Called "God"	Heb. 1:8
Exodus 3:2, 5, 6, 14	Claimed to Be "I Am"	John 8:58
Judges 13:15, 18	His Name Was "Wonderful"	Isa. 9:6
Exodus 23:20	Sent from God	John 5:30; 6:38
Exodus 14:19	Guides God's People	Matt. 28:20
Isa. 63:9	Loved and Redeemed His Own	Eph. 5:25
Joshua 5:13-15	Commander of Lord's Army	Rev. 19:11-14

It is important to notice that the "angel of the LORD" is both *identified with the Lord (Jehovah),* as in most of the passages quoted in the chart, and yet is *distinguished from the Lord.* In Isaiah 63:9, for example, the angel is distinguished from the Lord as "the angel of his presence" (v. 9). In Genesis 24:7 the angel is "sent" from God, and in Zechariah 1:12 there is a conversation between the "Lord" and the "angel of the Lord." That this angel of the Lord is Christ in the Old Testament is clear from the fact that He is distinguished from God, sent from God, does the work of redeeming and guiding His people, all of which are the ministries of Christ as known from the New Testament. And once Christ is born, the angel of the Lord no longer appears.

CONCLUSION

It has been contended that Christ is the key to the *interpretation* of the Old Testament Scriptures on the basis that Jesus five times affirmed that He was the fulfillment or message of the Old Testament. Upon examining these passages, it was concluded that there are four senses or ways in which Christ is the fulfillment of the Old Testament. He is the fulfillment of:

1. Old Testament Messianic prophecy (as illustrated in Luke and Acts)
2. Old Testament Levitical priesthood (as illustrated in Hebrews)
3. Old Testament moral precepts (as illustrated in Matthew)
4. Old Testament salvation promises (as illustrated in John)

Each of these views presents a different aspect of the ministry of Christ, respectively:

1. Messianic prophecy sees Him as Messiah and King
2. Levitical priesthood, as Priest and Sacrifice
3. Moral precepts, as Prophet and Teacher
4. Salvation promises, as Lord and Saviour

We may conclude, then, that there are several legitimate Christocentric interpretations to the Old Testament, but there are *no legitimate nonchristocentric approaches to the Old Testament.* Jesus said, "If you believed Moses, you would believe me, for he wrote of me. But if you do not believe his writings, how will you believe my words?" (John 5:46-47).[6]

[6]It should be noted here that Jesus' claim to be the fulfillment of Old Testament prophecies was not forced, as though He were trying, either deliberately or deceptively, to make the events of His life correspond to the predictions about the Messiah. In fact, many of the Messianic prophecies which were fulfilled in the life of Jesus of Nazareth were beyond His human control altogether, such as (1) the place of His birth (Micah 5:2); (2) the time (Dan. 9:25 ff.) and manner of His birth (Isa. 7:14); His flight into Egypt (Hosea 11:1); His childhood in Nazareth (Isa. 11:1, cf. Matt. 2:23); or even the manner of His death (Ps. 22:16) and subsequent piercing (Zech. 12:10). Even on the occasions where Jesus was conscious of bringing to pass the prophecies of the Old Testament (e.g., Matt. 3:15; 5:17; 26:54), there is no evidence that He manipulated events to demonstrate His Messianic credentials. On the contrary, Jesus carefully avoided any fanfare about the fulfillment of prophecy or His own Messianic identity. At His baptism it was not He but the voice from heaven that announced Him as the Son of God (Matt. 3:17). His transfiguration was performed only for the private audience of three of His closest disciples (Matt. 17:1 ff.). When men would discover for themselves that He was the Messiah, Jesus "charged them that they should tell no man . . . till the Son of man were risen from the dead" (Mark 9:9, AV). On some occasions Jesus evaded direct answers to the clear-cut question as to whether or not He was the Messiah (John 18:33 ff.; Matt. 11:4-5). When Jesus did give direct statements about His Messiahship they were given in private (cf. John 4:26) or only to His disciples (cf. John 16:28-29). Jesus did claim to be the Messiah and the Son of God, but He never paraded any prophetic pretensions nor did He ever attempt to force the events of His life to fit the fulfillment of Messianic prophecy.

3

CHRIST IN BOTH TESTAMENTS

Since Christ is the theme of the whole Old Testament as He Himself affirmed five times (Matt. 5:17; Luke 24:27, 44; John 5:39; Heb. 10:7), then the relationship between the Old and New Testaments is inseparably connected in the person of Christ. It is the exploration of this relation which is the subject of the present chapter. If Christ is the "binding" of the book of Scripture, then it will be impossible to understand the whole Bible without a knowledge of the relation of its two basic parts. How, then, are the two Testaments related?

OVERALL RELATIONSHIP BETWEEN OLD AND NEW TESTAMENTS

The overall relationship between the Testaments is one of mutual interdependence. The Old Testament is incomplete without the New. What the Old Testament prepared for, the New Testament provides in Christ. Christ is the anticipation of the Old and the realization of the New. For what is commenced in the Old Testament is completed in the New Testament, and the fact of Christ in the New Testament cannot be understood apart from the foundation laid for Him in the Old Testament. This relationship of mutual interdependence can be outlined as follows:

54

CHRIST IN BOTH TESTAMENTS

In	Old Test— Anticipation	New Test— Realization
Matt. 5:17	concealed contained the precept	revealed explained its perfection
Heb. 10:7	in shadow in ritual in picture	in substance in reality in person
Luke 24:27, 44 John 5:39	as foretold in prophecy In preincarnations	as fulfilled in history in the incarnation

The relationships between the Testaments may be divided generally into three classes corresponding with the broad ways in which Christ is contained in the Old Testament.[1] In each case the first two comparisons listed above are roughly synonymous, but since they do carry a different shade of meaning they are listed separately so as to further the elucidation of the comparison between the Testaments.

Christ Is Concealed in the Old and Revealed in the New

"The New is in the Old concealed, and the Old is in the New revealed," said Augustine. Or, as another has put it, the New is in the Old enfolded, and the Old is in the New unfolded. Now there is no problem in seeing Christ in the New Testament: the Gospels present Him as Prophet to His people; Acts and the Epistles reveal Him as the Priest for His people, at the right hand of God; and Revelation forecasts that He will be the King over all His people.

THE REASON CHRIST IS OFTEN MISSED IN THE OLD TESTAMENT

However, on the surface, it is not so clear that Christ is

[1] This third relationship combines the third and fourth Christocentric approaches mentioned in chapter 2, since Christ as Messiah and as Saviour are closely connected.

the theme of the whole Old Testament. In fact, Christ is *concealed* in the Old Testament. That Christ is not obvious on the pages of the Old Testament may be witnessed to by both Jews and Christians. While many Jews fail to find Christ in the Old Testament because of judicial blindness (II Cor. 3:14-16), many Christians fail to see Christ in the Old Testament simply because of scriptural ignorance. Of the Jews' failure to see Jesus in their Scriptures, Paul wrote: "But their minds were hardened; for to this day, when they read the old covenant, that same veil remains unlifted, because only through Christ is it taken away . . . . but when a man turns to the Lord the veil is removed" (II Cor. 3:14, 16).

The Christians have their minds opened to Christ and should not have the problem of seeing Him concealed in the canon of the Old Testament. Despite this fact, Jesus had to say to two of His disciples, "O foolish men, and slow of heart to believe all that the prophets have spoken! . . . And beginning with Moses and all the prophets, he *interpreted to them* in all the scriptures the things concerning himself" (Luke 24:25, 27). And later, to the other disciples, "he opened their minds to understand the scriptures" (Luke 24:45). Christ was *concealed* in the Old Testament, but this was then *revealed* to the disciples in the New Testament.

CONTAINED IN THE OLD AND EXPLAINED IN THE NEW

The truth of the two Testaments is related morally, for the New Testament *explains* the precepts which the Old Testament *contains*. For example, the Old Testament had taught the permanence of marriage, which because men had distorted, Moses had permitted to be dissolved (Deut. 24:1-4). On this basis the "Pharisees came up to him and tested him by asking, 'Is it lawful to divorce one's wife for *any cause?*'" (Matt. 19:3). Since Moses' "concession" had been misconstrued as God's "commandment," Jesus reaffirmed the true teaching of the Old Testament on marriage by saying, "But from the beginning it was not so" (Matt. 19:8). The Old

Testament was against divorce because God had joined man and wife in a hallowed union (Matt. 19:5). Malachi quotes the Lord as saying, "I hate divorce, . . . So take heed to yourselves and do not be faithless" (2:16). So the moral truth about marriage contained in the Old Testament, but obscured by tradition, is reaffirmed and more fully *explained* by Christ in the New Testament. Christ reaffirmed the ideal of the law by bringing out its divinely intended meaning.

PRECEPTS OF OLD ARE BROUGHT TO PERFECTION IN THE NEW

Not only did Jesus *reaffirm* the true meaning of the Old Testament morality, but He *transcended* it. According to Jesus the true essence of Old Testament morality is to "love the Lord your God with all your heart, and . . . . your neighbor as yourself," for "on these two commandments depend all the law and the prophets" (Matt. 22:37, 39-40). Now this truth is certainly contained in the Old Testament, but it is more fully explained in the New Testament. For example, the whole second table of commandments implies that one is to have another's interest at heart (cf. Exodus 20:12-17). There were regulations on how to treat servants (Exodus 21), the respect that must be paid to a neighbor's property (Exodus 22), and the love for one's enemies (Exodus 23, cf. Jonah 4:10-11) and even love for those who are "down and out" (cf. Hosea 3:1 ff.).

Love was truly *contained* in the Old Testament, but it was most fully *explained* in the New Testament. The Jews of Jesus' day had obscured the meaning of this commandment by questioning, "And who is my neighbor?" (Luke 10:29). Jesus answered by telling the story of the good Samaritan, who "proved *neighbor* to the man who fell among the robbers" (10:36). In other words, Jesus pointed out that men should not try to evade loving others as themselves by limiting the definition of the word *neighbor* and thereby implying that one need not love those who are not his neighbors.

But Jesus not only brought out the true meaning of the law in terms of love, He also fulfilled or perfected the meaning of the law by placing love on an even higher level. The law said love others *as* yourself; Jesus showed in His death that one can love others *more* than oneself. "Greater love has no man than this, that a man lay down his life for his friends" (John 15:13). And "in this is love perfected with us, . . . because as he is so are we in this world" (I John 4:17). So the *precepts* of love from the Old Testament are not only re-affirmed by Jesus but are transcended in the *perfect* love of the New Testament.

The Old Testament law had punishments connected with it, and hence, fear of the consequences of disobedience. The New Testament idea of love elevates the motivation for love and therefore eliminates the need of fear. "For fear has to do with punishment, and he who fears is not perfected in love" (I John 4:18). Once Jesus had shown, by His teaching and *by His own life and death for sinners,* that one ought to love others *more than* oneself, and not merely *as much as* oneself, love was lifted from the level of natural or *reciprocal* morality to the supernatural plane of sacrificial ethics. That is, once love was lifted from the level of "I love you because this is what I want you to do to *me*" to the higher plane of "I love you because God first loved me," then love could be perfected and fear could be cast out. For if one has this "perfect love," he no longer operates on the plane of reciprocal consequences but on the plateau of divine constraint. As John put it, "Beloved, if God so loved us, we also ought to love one another" (I John 4:11) or, again, "By this we know love, that he laid down his life for us; and we ought to lay down our lives for the brethren" (I John 3:16).

So the Old and New Testaments are inseparably connected in the moral concept of love. But the precept of reciprocal love in the Old Testament is *perfected* in the sacrificial love Jesus demonstrated in the New Testament.

CHRIST: FROM THE SHADOWS OF THE OLD TESTAMENT
TO THE SUBSTANCE OF THE NEW TESTAMENT

There is another tie between the Testaments. It is found in the relationship between *type* and *antitype*: between the *shadows* of Christ in the Old Testament and the *substance* of Christ in the New Testament.

FROM FORESHADOW TO FULFILLMENT

Hebrews stresses this connection between the Levitical priesthood and that of Christ's. We read, "The law has but a *shadow* of the good things to come instead of the true form of these *realities*" (Heb. 10:1). That is, the ceremonies of the Old Testament only *foreshadowed* what Christ Himself *fulfilled* (cf. chap. 2). This is why Hebrews can present the substance or true realities of Christ as *better than:*

1. the angels (1:4)
2. the Old Testament hope (7:19)
3. the old covenant (7:22)
4. the former promises (8:6)
5. the Old Testament sacrifices (9:23)
6. their earthly country (hope and destiny) (11:16)
7. the old possessions (10:34)
8. the Old Testament resurrection (11:35)

And because of these things, the writer of Hebrews says, "We feel sure of *better things* that belong to salvation" (6:9) because "God had foreseen *something better* for us, that apart from us they [the Old Testament believers] should not be made perfect" (11:40). So the shadow of the Old must give way to the substance of the perfect and permanent reality in Christ.

It is for this reason that Hebrews can speak of the temporality of:

1. the Aaronic priesthood—which needed a "change" (7:12)
2. the Aaronic priests—who "serve a copy and shadow of the heavenly" (8:5)

3. the law—which had also "necessarily a change" (7:12)
4. the tabernacle—which was only a "pattern" of the real (8:5)
5. the sacrifices—which were "abolished" (10:9)
6. the old covenant—which was not "faultless" (8:7) and so is "obsolete" and will "vanish way" (8:13)

And since the shadow of the old covenant was only temporal, the substance of the new, in order to abolish the old, must be *final*. So it is that Hebrews is able to speak of *eternal*:

> salvation (5:9)
> judgment (6:2)
> redemption (9:12)
> Spirit (9:14)
> inheritance (9:15)
> covenant (13:20)

All of this permanence is because Christ is the High Priest who fulfills the Levitical system, has a throne (1:8), priesthood (5:6; 7:20), consecration (7:28), and glory (13:21) which last *forever*.

FROM RITUAL TO REALITY

What has been said about the priesthood, sacrifices and temple of the Old Testament may also be said of the sabbaths and festivals. "These are only a *shadow* of what is to come; but the *substance* belongs to Christ" (Col. 2:17). Once the *reality* has come, the *ritual* which prefigured it is no longer needed. In other words, the *types* of the Old Testament are fulfilled in the *truth* of the New Testament.

Since a Christocentric interpretation of the feast was discussed in the preceding chapter, it will be sufficient here to say that Christ fulfills and transcends the Levitical ritual of the Old Testament as a man transcends his own shadow at midday. It is only when the prophetic light was rising that the shadows of Christ were long. Once the full light had come, the shadows disappeared. Paul's argument in Colossians was for the dissolution in Christ of all Old Testament ritualistic ceremonies separating believers. Christ has "canceled the bond which stood against us with its legal demands; this he set aside, nailing it to the cross" (Col. 2:14). "Why," Paul asked, "do you submit to regulations, 'Do not handle, Do not taste, Do not touch' . . . . they are of no value in checking the indulgence of the flesh" (Col. 2:20-23). The New Testament believer has died to the demands of the law (3:2) and has been raised above these *rituals* to a new *reality* in Christ and, therefore, should "seek the things which are above" (3:1).

Christ in Picture and in Person

There are many fitting pictures of Christ in the Old Testament which, properly speaking, should not be classified as types. For a type not only *pictured* Christ but it was a kind of implicit prediction that Christ would fulfill its function.[2] Such were the sacrifices, the temple, the priesthood, and the feasts of the old economy. They were *prefigurations* that were not permanent but pointed to their perfection in Christ. But, besides these types, there are in the Old Testament many *pictures* which are appropriately applied to Christ. Some of these the New Testament applies to Christ and some it does not. In the former class are:

1. Jonah's three days and nights in the whale (Matt. 12:40)
2. Solomon and his wisdom (Matt. 12:42)

[2]The Greek word for *type* (*typos*), usually translated "example" (I Tim. 4:12), does not have a technical meaning in the New Testament and is used of Christ only once (Rom. 5:14), where Adam is said to be a "type" of Christ. What is meant by a type of Christ is sometimes called "copies" (*hypodeigma*) (Heb. 8:5; 9:23) and sometimes even "symbolical" (*parabole*) (Heb. 9:9) and even antitype or "copy" (*antitypos*) (Heb. 9:24). These words have a wide variety of meaning including "print of the nails" (John 20:25), "warning" (I Cor. 10:11), or "figures" (idols) (Acts 7:43) and therefore what is meant by a "type" cannot be decided from New Testament usage. On the basis of a general rule of interpretation, it would seem to be better to restrict the meaning of *type* to Old Testament persons, institutions, and ceremonies which were divinely appointed prefigurations of what Christ would later fulfill. Everything else that may be fittingly applied to Christ (whether the New Testament applies it or not) would then be called a *picture* or illustration of Christ.

3. the "Rock" in the wilderness (I Cor. 10:4)
4. the "manna" from heaven (John 6:41)
5. the "serpent" in the wilderness (John 3:14)

It is difficult to draw a distinct line this side of religious fancy in regard to pictures of Christ in the Old Testament which are not applied to Him by the New Testament. On the other hand, as with typology, it would seem too restrictive to limit "pictures" of Christ to only those things in the Old Testament which the New Testament applies to Christ. It would be better to use the *general principle* involved in the above list, namely, anything which appropriately depicts some significant aspect of Christ's Messianic mission and which has some matching Messianic metaphor in the Bible. The following are some suggested *pictures* of Christ in the Old Testament:

1. Noah's ark of safety (Gen. 7; cf. I Peter 3:21)
2. Isaac, the sacrifice (Gen. 22; cf. John 3:16, Heb. 11:19)
3. Jacob's ladder from earth to heaven (Gen. 28; cf. John 1:51; 14:6)
4. Joseph, rejected by his brethren (Gen. 37; cf. John 1:10-11)
5. cities of refuge (Deut. 4, 19; cf. I Peter 5:7; Matt. 11:28)
6. kinsman redeemer (Ruth 4; cf. Gal. 3:13)
7. beloved, etc. (Song of Solomon; cf. Eph. 5:25)

There are many beautiful pictures of Christ in the Song of Solomon, such as "chiefest among ten thousand" (5:10, ASV), "the finest gold" (5:11), and "altogether lovely" (5:16, ASV). However, religious fancy added to extreme typology and allegory have too often considered this canticle, in all of its details, a type of Christ's love for the church. It would appear better to consider this love poem to be an *illustration*, rather than a typological prediction of Christ.

Whatever status one gives to these "pictures" of Christ in the Old Testament, whether that of a typological prediction or an illustration, it must be agreed that the resemblance of the *picture* in the Old Testament falls far short of the reality of the *person* in the New Testament. The Old Testament gives many portraits of Christ; it is a kind of Messianic picture album, but the New Testament presents the Christ of the portraits.

CHRIST: FORETOLD IN THE OLD TESTAMENT AND FULFILLED IN THE NEW TESTAMENT

There is a third sense in which the two Testaments are related, namely, as what is *foretold* about Christ to what is *fulfilled* in Christ. This, of course, is the significance of Messianic prophecy. There were many Messianic promises from Genesis (3:15) to Malachi (4:2), some of which have already been discussed (chap. 2).

FROM PROPHECY TO HISTORY

The New Testament relates to the Old the way history relates to its prophecy. Now there were many "predictions" made about Christ in the Old Testament, some more explicit than others. These Old Testament prophecies may be viewed as fulfilled in Christ in at least three different ways:

1. Some prophecies were *directly predictive* of Christ and therefore may rightly apply to Him, as the New Testament usually does.[3]
2. Other prophecies were not directly predictive of Christ but were applied to Him by the New Testament because they were *Messianic in principle.*
3. There were "prophecies" *neither predictive nor applied to Christ* by the New Testament, but because they "picture" what He accomplished in the same way as the passages which were Messianic in principle, they may be

[3]There is probably a fourth kind of Messianic prophecy, namely, predictive but not applied to Christ by the New Testament, because they had no occasion to do so. Perhaps the "star of Jacob" in Num. 24:17 is an example of this kind. No doubt Gen. 49:10 fits this classification as well. Of course, most of the predictive prophecy about Christ's second coming would fit into this category.

63

appropriately applied to Christ. These are called "Messianic pictures" to distinguish them from "Messianic principles."

FULFILLMENT OF MESSIANIC PREDICTIONSFULFILLMENT OF MESSIANIC PREDICTIONS

First, there were many events that were the fulfillment of direct *predictions* about the coming Messiah or Saviour. For example, it was predicted that Christ would be:

1. born of a woman (Gen. 3:15)
2. through the line of Shem (Gen. 9:26)
3. from the seed of Abraham (Gen. 12:3; 15:5)
4. and from the seed of Isaac (Gen. 21:12)
5. and from the seed of Jacob (Gen. 26:4)
6. from the tribe of Judah (Gen. 49:10)
7. of the family of David (II Sam. 7:12)
8. from the sons of Solomon (I Chron. 28:4-7)
9. one who is born of a virgin (Isa. 7:14)
10. in the city of Bethlehem (Micah 5:2)
11. about 483 (years) from Nehemiah's time (444 B.C.; Dan. 9:25)
12. who shall ride as King into Jerusalem (Zech. 9:9)
13. suffer and die for men's sins (Isa. 53, cf. Ps. 22)
14. but rise from the dead (Ps. 2, 16)

FULFILLMENT OF MESSIANIC PRINCIPLES

Other prophecies, not directly predictive, were legitimately applied to Christ by the New Testament because they embodied a truth in the life of the prophet or people of the Messiah, which because of their preparatory mission in the Old Testament, could only find its full realization in the person of the Messiah Himself. Such prophecies are not said to be fulfilled in the New Testament in the sense of the coming to pass of a Messianic prediction but in the sense of the coming to perfection of a *Messianic principle.*

Now it is not always easy to determine what is predictive

and what is not because there is no infallible way of determining the difference. A suggested rule is this: if the passage, in its Old Testament context, was divinely intended to give information in advance about the coming Christ, then it is Messianic in the predictive sense (whether it is cited by the New Testament or not). On the other hand, if the passage in its context refers primarily to the historical, personal and/or national situation of the prophet and is not directed to their future, then it is probably only Messianic in principle.

Often there will be prophetic "indicators" if the passage is *predictive*. For example, the prophecy about the Son of David who would reign upon David's throne in II Samuel 7 was not merely a reference to David's son Solomon, because David recognized that the Lord had spoken of his dynasty "for a *great while* to come" (7:19). Often, too, the prophets will distinguish the future from the present by these phrases: "And it shall come to pass *afterward*" (Joel 2:28); "In *those days*, and at that time" (Joel 3:1); "And in *that day*" (Hosea 2:21); "It shall come to pass in the *latter days*" (Micah 4:1); "On that day" (Zech. 13:1), etc. Where indications that the prophecy is predictive are absent, it is often (at best) only *Messianic in principle*. The following are some examples of the New Testament fulfillment of this kind of *principle-prophecy*.

1. Christ's return from Egypt (Matt. 2:15, cf. Hosea 11:1)
2. Christ's living in Nazareth (Matt. 2:23, cf. Isa. 11:1)
3. Christ's parabolic method of teaching (Matt. 13:34-35, cf. Ps. 78:2)
4. the amount of Christ's betrayal money (Matt. 26:15, cf. Zech. 11:12)
5. Christ's betrayer would eat with Him (John 13:18, cf. Ps. 41:9)
6. Christ's enemies hated Him without cause (John 15:25, cf. Ps. 35:19)
7. Judas would be lost (John 17:12, cf. Ps. 41:9)

8. another would replace Judas (Acts 1:20, cf. Ps. 69:25; 109:8, ASV)

Besides the Messianic "principles," which are applied to Christ in the New Testament, there are other similar passages which the New Testament writers had no occasion to use (although they could have legitimately used them of Christ). These "Messianic pictures" were not predictive, but they are fitting expressions of what the Messiah actually did. They are metaphors taken from the life of the people of the Messianic nation that may be more perfectly applied to the person of the Messiah. For example, there is a pictorial fulfillment or perfection in Christ of:

1. giving His cheeks to the smiter (Lam. 3:30, cf. Matt. 27:30)
2. the sun darkened at noonday (Amos 8:9, cf. Matt. 27:45)
3. Israel mourning for an only son (Amos 8:10, cf. Luke 23:28)
4. offering vinegar to Christ on the cross (Ps. 69:21, cf. Matt. 27:48)
5. wisdom personified (Prov. 8, cf. I Cor. 1:30; Col. 2:3)

Much of the exaggeration and fancy in Messianic study might better be reduced to this category and recognized as the fulfillment or perfection of "pictures" of Christ and not really predictions about Him at all. Even so, there should be some meaningful bounds to the Messianic metaphors applied to Christ. Perhaps the rule should be: any Old Testament passage may be appropriately applied to Christ, even though the New Testament writers did not apply it, providing that it exemplifies something from the life of the Messianic people which finds an actual correspondence with the truth about Christ presented somewhere in the Bible. Or, in other words, if the passage and principle involved in it are similar to those cited by New Testament writers, then it may be legitimately attributed to Him.

Perhaps the difficulty of determining what kind of prophecy a given passage is can be better appreciated if it is remembered that the prophets themselves searched their own writings to find "what *person* or *time* was indicated by the Spirit of Christ within them" (I Peter 1:11). That is, the truth about Christ was often only *implicit* in the prophetic writings and was not made explicit until the New Testament. Jesus provided an example of this when He quoted Isaiah 61:1-2 and stopped in the middle of the verse, declaring to the people that "today this scripture has been fulfilled in your hearing" (Luke 4:21). The very next phrase, which Jesus did not read, says, "And the day of the vengeance of our God . . . ." This referred to Christ's *second* coming, and so He did not quote it as fulfilled in His *first* coming. The valley of time between the two mountain peaks of truth about Christ's comings was not clearly revealed in the Old Testament. As a result, much of the prophetic truth *enfolded* in the Old Testament was not *unfolded* until the New Testament.

FROM PREINCARNATION TO THE INCARNATION

Finally, there is another relationship between the Old and New Testaments on the Messianic level: in the Old Testament there were *preincarnations* of Christ, and in the New Testament there is *the incarnation* of Christ. The Old Testament appearances of Christ (or Christophanies) have already been discussed (in chap. 2) under the treatment of "the angel of the LORD." Here it will be briefly noted how the incarnation of Christ in the New Testament relates to and supersedes these preincarnate appearances in the Old Testament.

For one thing, these Old Testament appearances were only *occasional* (Gen. 16, 22, 31, 48; Exodus 3; Joshua 5; Judges 2, 6, 13; II Kings 1, 19), whereas in the New Testament Christ's presence is *continual*. In addition, these preincarnations of Christ were only *temporary*, but His incarnation is *perma-*

nent. The angel of the Lord appeared only periodically before Christ's birth and does not appear at all after Christ is born.[4] But once Christ assumed flesh, He became the God-Man forever. John said, "And the Word [Christ] became flesh and dwelt among us" (1:14). Hebrews says, "Since therefore the children share in flesh and blood, he himself [Christ] likewise partook of the same nature" (2:14). Christ's resurrection from the dead was a *bodily* one (cf. Luke 24:39), as was His ascension into heaven (Acts 1:9-11). And in His present session at the right hand of God, Christ still retains union with His body. Colossians 2:9 says of the ascended Christ, "For in him the whole fulness of deity dwells [present tense] *bodily.*" And, according to prophecy, Christ shall return to this earth bodily and reign forever (Acts 1:11, cf. Zech. 14:4, etc.). Paul wrote of Christ, "He was manifested in the *flesh*" (I Tim. 3:16), and John considered it a heresy to deny Christ's humanity, saying, "Every spirit which confesses that Jesus Christ has come *in the flesh* is of God, and every spirit which does not confess Jesus is not of God" (I John 4:2-3).

It should be pointed out that the incarnation of Christ was not merely an "appearance" of flesh; it was a "manifestation" in the flesh. Christ did not have merely the "form" of flesh but He *was* flesh in the same respect as we are, "yet without sinning" (Heb. 4:15). It is only in this latter sense that Christ's humanity is said to be "in the *likeness* of men" (Phil. 2:7). Christ's human nature was *unlike* ours only in that it was without sin; in every other point it was exactly the same as ours (Rom. 8:3).

Now this kind of incarnation transcends the Old Testament preincarnations not only in that it is continual, permanent

---

[4]*An* angel of the Lord (Gabriel) appeared to Joseph (Matt. 1:20); *an* angel of the Lord spoke to Philip (Acts 8:26); and *an* angel of the Lord released Peter (Acts 12:7), but not *the* angel of the Lord. Furthermore, the New Testament "angel of the Lord," unlike "the angel of the LORD" in the Old Testament, did not permit worship of himself (cf. Rev. 22:8-9), but "the angel of the LORD" in the Old Testament demanded worship (cf. Exodus 3:5; Joshua 5:15).

and truly human but in that it is also superior to the Old Testament means of revelation. In the Old Testament God revealed Himself in *laws,* but in the New Testament He is revealed in the *life* of Christ. "He who has seen me has seen the Father," Jesus declared (John 14:9). God revealed Himself in *propositions* in the Old Testament, but in Christ, God's revelation is in a *Person.* The Old Testament revelation was also in *symbols* (tabernacle, sacrifices, etc.), but in these last days He has spoken through His *Son* (Heb. 1:1-2).

Summary

Christ at once sums up in Himself the perfection of the Old Testament precepts, the substance of Old Testament shadows and types, and the fulfillment of Old Testament forecasts. Those truths about Him which bud forth in the Old Testament come into full bloom in the New Testament; the flashlight of prophetic truth turns into the floodlight of divine revelation. The Old Testament foreshadows find their fulfillment in the New Testament in several ways: (1) The *moral precepts* of the Old Testament become fulfilled or perfected in the life and teachings of Christ. (2) The *ceremonial* and *typical* truths were only shadows of the true substance to be found in Christ. (3) The *Messianic prophecies* foretold in the Old Testament were finally fulfilled in the history of the New Testament. In each of these relationships it can be seen that the Testaments are inseparably connected. The New is not only supplementary to the Old but it is the necessary complement to it. As the book of Hebrews puts it, "God had foreseen something better for us, that apart from us they [Old Testament believers] should not be made perfect" (Heb. 11:40). For what was contained in the Old Testament is fully explained only in the New Testament.

4

CHRIST IN EVERY SECTION OF
THE BIBLE

One may spend his time in typology and prophecy, attempting to discover what Jesus meant when He claimed to be the theme of the whole Bible, and miss a most obvious point—that Christ is also the key to the *structural tie* of the Bible. Christ, viewed as the structural tie between the two Testaments, has already been discussed in the previous chapter; here Christ will be presented as the theme that unites the various *sections* of the Bible.

A FOURFOLD CHRISTOCENTRIC STRUCTURE OF SCRIPTURE

TWO DIVISIONS OF THE OLD TESTAMENT

From most ancient times the Bible was divided into basic sections. One of the most common of these divisions, and possibly the earliest one, was a twofold division of the Old Testament into Law and Prophets. The Law, which Moses wrote, was placed in a class by itself, and everything that came after this was called the Prophets.

The Law of Moses. That Moses wrote the Law and that it was placed in a class by itself is evident from the testimony of a long line of biblical successors to Moses.

First, it should be noted that *Moses* claimed to write the Law as God revealed it to him (cf. Exodus 20:1; 35:1; Num. 1:1; 36:13). He warned the people to "not add to the word which I command you, nor take from it" (Deut. 4:2). And "when Moses had finished writing the words of this law in a book, to the very end, Moses commanded the Levites, . . . 'Take this book of the law, and put it by the side of the ark of the covenant of the Lord your God' " (Deut. 31:24-26).

Joshua and his successors considered Moses' Law to be sacred and divinely authoritative: (1) *Joshua*, at the beginning of his ministry, enjoined the Law of Moses to the people (Joshua 1:7-8), and urged them at the end of his days "to keep and do all that is written in the book of the law of Moses" (23:6). (2) In *Judges* the Law of Moses continues to be recognized (3:4) as well as in *Ruth* (cf. 4:1-12). (3) In the time of *I and II Samuel*, Moses' Law is referred to as the Law of the Lord and of Moses (I Chron. 16:40; 22:12). (4) *I and II Kings* continue the recognition of Moses' Law (I Kings 2:3; II Kings 18:6). (5) At the time of the Babylonian captivity both *Jeremiah* (8:8; 15:1) and *Daniel* (9:11) refer to the Law of Moses, and (6) after the exile the Levitical system is reinstituted "as it is written in the book of Moses" (*Ezra* 6:18), and the priests of *Nehemiah's* day, "read from the book of Moses in the hearing of the people" (Neh. 13:1). Finally, *Malachi*, the last of the Old Testament prophets, admonished the people to "remember the law of my servant Moses" (4:4). One would conclude from this that throughout the Old Testament Moses' books were recognized by the people of God, placed in a class by themselves, and preserved as the "sacred" Word of God.

The Prophets after Moses. Moses' books were placed in a class of their own because he was the common author and the great lawgiver of Israel. But after Moses there were other "prophets" who also wrote divinely inspired books.

Joshua, for example, wrote his words in a "book" called "the law of God" (Joshua 24:26) in order that the people might hear "all the words of the Lord which he spoke" to Joshua (v. 27). Although Joshua called his book "the *law* of God," as indeed the whole Old Testament is sometimes referred to as "Law" (cf. Matt. 5:18; John 15:25; Acts 25:8), nevertheless, he begins a section of the Old Testament which becomes distinguished from the "Law of Moses" and is called "the Prophets."

This distinction between "Moses" and the "Prophets" is made even in Old Testament times. As early as the time of captivity (sixth century, B. C.), Daniel referred to "the law of Moses" (9:11, 13) and "the books" (9:2), among which was the "word of the LORD to Jeremiah the prophet" (9:2). This would seem to indicate that "Moses" and the "Prophets" were placed in two different categories. In the postcaptivity period (fifth century, B.C.), Zechariah refers to the stubborn people who would not "hear the *law* [of Moses] and the words which the LORD of hosts had sent by his Spirit through the *former prophets*" (7:12, cf. 1:4; 7:7). Nehemiah (9:26) makes a similar distinction, saying "they were disobedient . . . and cast thy *law* behind their back and killed thy *prophets*" (cf. 9:30).[1]

This same twofold division of "Law and Prophets" continued between the Testaments, for example, in the Dead Sea Scroll *Manual of Discipline*,[2] and in the intertestamental religious literature (cf. II Macc. 15:9).

In the New Testament, the twofold division of "Law and Prophets" is one of the most common ways of referring to the Old Testament. It occurs twelve times (cf. Matt. 5:17; 7:12; Luke 24:27). In this last passage "Law and Prophets" are defined as "all the scriptures" and, in Luke 16:16, as everything inspired of God, from Moses to John the Baptist.

TWO DIVISIONS OF THE NEW TESTAMENT

The Four Gospels. If the Old Testament is viewed as Law and Prophets, the New Testament may be similarly divided into Gospels and Epistles, with Acts and Revelation included in the latter category. The four Gospels naturally stand first

[1]In Ezra 9:11 the word *prophets* is used to include Moses (cf. Deut. 18: 15) and the other prophets after him, just as the word *Law* is sometimes used to include the writings of the prophets as well as Moses (see above).

[2]Late second century, B.C., I, 3; VIII, 15.

in the order of New Testament books, because they give the life, teaching, death and resurrection of Christ, which formed the basis for the church, about which the Epistles later speak.

The Epistles. The rest of the New Testament is related to the Gospels as the apostles were related to Christ. The Gospels record what Jesus taught, and the Epistles record what the apostles taught about Him. In this respect then, the Old Testament is divided into Moses and the Prophets and the New Testament into Christ and the "Apostles." And to develop this relationship, it may be noted that the Epistles are to the Gospels what the Prophets were to the Law. The latter in each case is the structure built on the foundation of the former.

CHRIST IN THE FOURFOLD DIVISION OF THE BIBLE

Since Christ has been found to be the theme of the whole Bible (see chaps. 2-3), it will follow that He is the theme of each part. In fact, since Christ is the unity that makes a whole out of the parts of Scripture, then however the Bible is divided, one must seek to relate the sections to a Christocentric structure. If a fourfold division is followed, then Christ may be seen as the unfolding theme that binds the whole Bible together in the following way:

One Theme	Twofold Structure	Fourfold Structure
Christ	Anticipation of Christ (O. T.)	Law—Foundation for Christ
		Prophets—Expectation of Christ
	Realization of Christ (N. T.)	Gospels—Manifestation of Christ
		Epistles—Interpretation of Christ

Law: The Foundation for Christ. Moses and his Law are to the Old Testament what Christ and His gospel are to the

New Testament, namely, the *foundation* of all that follows. In fact, the Bible compares Moses and Christ in several basic ways in this regard. First, John says, "For the law was given through Moses; grace and truth came through Jesus Christ" (John 1:17). Now as Moses' Law was fundamental to the message of the prophets to follow him, so is the grace and truth of Christ's gospel the basis of the apostles' message.

Furthermore, both Moses and Christ were mediators of covenants; Moses mediated the old covenant (or testament)[3] and Christ is the Mediator of the new covenant (Heb. 8:6; Gal. 3:19). The Israelites, who were delivered by Moses, are said to have been "baptized into Moses" (I Cor. 10:2), as Christians are said to be "baptized into Christ" (Rom. 6:3). Finally, both shared in the radiation of God's glory (II Cor. 3:7; John 1:14). The position of Moses and his Law in the Old Testament was fundamental to what followed in the Old Testament, even as what Christ taught in the New Testament was essential to the truth of the rest of the New Testament.

Moses' Law laid the foundation for Christ in several ways:

1. By way of *prefiguration*, the Law of Moses laid down the basic types and patterns which were later fulfilled in Christ (see chap. 2).
2. By way of moral *preparation*, the Law of Moses tutored men in the basics of right and wrong until their guilt led them to Christ for forgiveness (cf. Gal. 3:19-24; Rom. 3:19-22).
3. By way of *prophecy*, the Law of Moses recorded the first and most basic Messianic hopes to the people of Israel (cf. Gen. 3:15; 49:10; Deut. 18:15).

The Prophets: The Expectation for Christ. Since the Law of Moses had laid the foundation for Christ in these three bas-

---

[3]The word *testament* in the Bible means an agreement or arrangement between two parties and should usually be translated "covenant" (as it is in ASV and RSV), since the word *testament* means a "will," which needs only the action of one person.

ic ways, it was natural that those who came after him would look forward in *expectation* to the fulfillment of these hopes. Moses had promised Israel, "The LORD your God will raise up for you a prophet like me from among you, from your brethren" (Deut. 18:15). And all of the writings after Moses, in one way or another, amplified this expectation.

In Joshua the hope was high since the people possessed the land which God had promised them in preparation for their Messianic mission. In Judges there were many deliverers and saviors (e.g., Gideon, Barak, Samson), but *the* Saviour did not appear. Samuel held out the hope more clearly in the establishing of a kingdom, the anointing of King David, through whom the "anointed One" (Messiah) was promised to come (II Sam. 7:12 ff.). At first in Kings the Messianic expectation was at a peak, but it soon declined in the polygamy, idolatry, and final disunity of the great Solomonic empire. As the empire of Israel degenerated, the prophets (Isaiah, Jeremiah, Ezekiel, Daniel and the Twelve) kept the fires of Messianic expectation burning to the very last chapter of the Old Testament (Mal. 4:2). Their expectation was accentuated by Judah's return from the Babylonian captivity, recorded in Ezra, and the national reconstruction related in Nehemiah. Of course, Israel's poets had also added to this expectation by their many spiritual aspirations and, sometimes, even Messianic predictions.

The Gospels: The Manifestation of Christ. It was the Prophet Isaiah, in his expectation of Christ, who said the Messiah would be introduced by "the voice of one crying in the wilderness: Prepare the way of the Lord" (Matt. 3:3, from Isa. 40:3). And as the New Testament opens, this is exactly what John the Baptist is doing. When John is asked why he is heralding Christ, he replies: "That he [Christ] should be made *manifest* to Israel" (John 1:31, ASV). In other words, the One for whom Moses laid the foundation and to whom the prophets looked in expectation had come in a historic and personal manifestation. In Christ the anticipation of the Old Testament becomes the realization of the New Testament. Prophecy becomes history, as the Logos (Christ) comes into the cosmos, or world (John 1:14).

Why this manifestation of Christ in the world? The New Testament gives many important answers to this question. (1) Peter said Christ "was made *manifest* at the end of the times . . . so that your faith and hope may be in God" (I Peter 1:20-21). (2) John wrote "that he was *manifested* to take away sins" (I John 3:5, ASV), and (3) "to this end was the Son of God *manifested*, that he might destroy the works of the devil" (I John 3:8, ASV), or (4) to show that "the love of God was made *manifest* among us, . . . so that we might live through him" (I John 4:9). (5) Paul says Christ came to *manifest* to His saints the "mystery hidden for ages and ages" (Col. 1:26). (6) Elsewhere, Paul writes of the salvation and calling of the believer, which is now "*manifested* through the appearing of our Savior Christ Jesus" (II Tim. 1:9-10). (7) Jesus described the purpose of His appearing in these words to His Father: "I have *manifested* thy name to the men whom thou gavest me out of the world" (John 17:6).

Christ was at first manifest to the world, "yet the world knew him not. He came to his own home, and his own people received him not" (John 1:10-11). This is why He then manifested Himself to His disciples and "to all who received him, who believed in his name, he gave power to become children of God" (John 1:12).

The Epistles (and Acts): The Interpretation of Christ. The Old Testament lays the foundation for Christ and looks forward to Him in expectation. The New Testament presents the historic manifestation of Christ in the Gospels. In the Epistles, the apostles give the official *interpretation* of Christ's appearance and its *application* to the life of the believers.

Jesus taught His apostles for three and a half years before His death and then for forty days after His resurrection (Acts 1:3), but He Himself did not write any interpretation of His mission. Jesus left this task to His apostles, with this promise: "The Holy Spirit, whom the Father will send in my name, he will teach you all things, and bring to your remembrance all that I have said to you" (John 14:26). The twenty-two epistles of the New Testament came in fulfillment of that promise. They are the record of apostolic *interpretation* of the manifestation of Jesus Christ in this world.

Before the apostles had recorded their authoritative interpretation of Christ's teachings, death, resurrection and ascension, the early church was guided by their living ministries: (1) The church from the first "devoted themselves to the apostles' teaching" (Acts 2:42), (2) Even "the [Holy] Spirit was given through the laying on of the apostles' hands" (Acts 8:18), (3) The great issues of the church were decided by the apostles' pronouncements (Acts 15:22 ff.), (4) The church was exhorted to "hold to the traditions which were taught" by the apostles (II Thess. 2:15), or (5) to remember the "commandment of the Lord and Savior through your apostles" (II Peter 3:2).

Once the living ministry of the apostles had ceased, the only authoritative interpretation of Christ was the apostolic writings of the New Testament. Even before the last apostle (John) died, there was a growing collection of their writings, which was considered by the church to be an authoritative interpretation of Christ. Peter tells of a collection of Paul's letters, which he included with the "other scriptures" (II Peter 3:15-16). Paul's writings were being read and circulated among the churches (Col. 4:16). Jude, one of the later New Testament books (probably written after Paul and Peter were martyred), quotes the Apostle Peter's letter (Jude 17-18). Gradually the living interpretation was replaced by the *written interpretation* of the New Testament. This does not mean that the written record was now "a matter of one's own *interpretation*, because no prophecy ever came by the impulse of man, but men moved by the Holy Spirit spoke from God" (II Peter 1:20-21). That is, the interpretation of

Christ is from the illumination of the Spirit of God through the Word of God. Christ said, "The scriptures, . . . bear witness to me," and "The Spirit . . . will guide you into all the truth" (John 5:39; 16:13).

A SIXFOLD CHRISTOCENTRIC STRUCTURE OF SCRIPTURE

THE BASIS OF A SIXFOLD DIVISION OF THE BIBLE

The foregoing analysis suggests how Christ may be related to the Scriptures when they are divided into four sections. However, from very early times, the Jews divided their Old Testament into three parts (later called Law, Prophets, Writings); and the New Testament may be given a corresponding threefold division, considering the book of Acts as separate from the Epistles, thus yielding a sixfold sectioning of the whole Bible.

As early as 200 B.C. the Hebrew Old Testament was sometimes divided into "the law and the prophets and the other books" (Prologue to Ecclesiasticus [Sirach]). We are not told which books were in which class, only that they contained "many great teachings" about Israel. Josephus (A.D. 37-100) is more specific in his threefold division of the Old Testament. He says there were five books of Moses, thirteen prophets, and "four books containing hymns to God."[4] However, the earliest testimony to the present-day threefold Hebrew division of the Old Testament is the Babylonian Talmud, which in its present form only dates back to the fifth century A.D. It lists the books as twenty-four in these three sections:

   I. Law—5
      Genesis—Deuteronomy

  II. Prophets—8
      Former Prophets—Joshua, Judges, Samuels, Kings
      Latter Prophets—Isaiah, Jeremiah, Ezekiel, Twelve
      (minor)

---

[4]Josephus, *Against Apion*, I, 8.

III. Writings—11
    Poets—Psalms, Proverbs, Job
    Rolls—Song of Solomon, Ruth, Lamentations, Esther,
      Ecclesiastes
    History—Daniel, Ezra-Nehemiah, Chronicles

The twofold division of the Old Testament had only Law and Prophets, since everyone who wrote after Moses had to be a "prophet" in the sense that he was one through whom God spoke.[5] In fact, all the writers of the Old Testament, including Moses, were called prophets (cf. Ezra 9:11; II Peter 1:20). But since Moses was the great deliverer, lawgiver, and prophet, his books were put in a class of their own, and the rest were called "Prophets." Just why or when the "Prophets" were first classed as "prophets and other books" or "prophets and books containing hymns to God" is not clear. Several solutions have been offered:

1. The books in the third class were not considered equally authoritative to the "Law and Prophets" and so were placed in a separate section.
2. The last section was last to be written and accepted into the canon and therefore stands at the end of the Old Testament.
3. Those books written by men who had only a prophetic *gift* but did not hold the prophetic *office* were placed in the third class by themselves.
4. The books of the third section were placed there for topical or for festal reasons (to be used in connection with the various feasts).

Generally, the first two reasons are supported by liberal scholars and the last two are held among conservative scholars. On the basis of Jesus' authority (cf. chap. 1), which is

[5]In this sense of the word *prophet,* even David (Acts 2:30) and Solomon (I Kings 4:29; 3:11) were prophets.

supported by Josephus, the first two positions are unacceptable.[6]

CHRIST IN THE SIXFOLD STRUCTURE

Whichever is the true reason that the Old Testament took on a threefold division, there is an indication that Jesus Himself recognized such a division on one occasion (Luke 24:44).[7] What is important is not how the Bible is divided but how it is related. If there are three sections, then all three sections must be related to Christ. This may be done in the manner shown in the accompanying chart.

Fourfold Structure	Sixfold·Structure
Law—Foundation for Christ	Law—Foundation for Christ
Prophets—Expectation of Christ	Prophets—Expectation of Christ
	Writings—Aspiration for Christ
Gospels—Manifestation of Christ	Gospels—Manifestation of Christ
Epistles—Interpretation of Christ	Acts—Propagation of Christ*
	Epistles—Interpretation of Christ

*This might also be called "Evangelization of Christ." See chap. 5.

The Aspiration and Expectation for Christ. A study of the chart will reveal that the sixfold structure involves only the subdividing of "Prophets" into "Prophets" and "Writings."

[6]For example, the book of Daniel, which is placed in "the writings" was not written late (e.g., second century, B.C.) because it *claims* to be a prediction of events before that time (cf. chaps. 2, 7). Jesus said Daniel was a "prophet" (Matt. 24:15), and Josephus apparently listed Daniel among the prophets, since Daniel is certainly not a "hymn." Then too there is good internal evidence that Job and many psalms were very early.

[7]It is commonly thought that Jesus, in referring to Law, Prophets and Psalms, verified the existence of a threefold division of the Old Testament. Psalms, since it is the first and largest book of the section, is supposed to stand for the whole section.

This division lends itself well to a Christ-centered structural approach because it separates poetry and prophecy, the former stressing—as poets are prone to do—the *aspiration,* and the latter emphasizing—as prophets should do—the *expectation* of Christ. As any division will be, this one is somewhat artificial since there is some great poetry in the Prophets (cf. Isaiah), and some great prophecies in the books of poetry (cf. Ps. 2, 16, 22). Be that as it may, the threefold division of the Old Testament does make overall sense on the Christocentric level. In fact, taken together with the Law, they present a three-directional anticipation for Christ in the Old Testament.

In the Law there is a *downward view* as the foundation is laid for Christ. It is downward insofar as the dominant action is from above and upon men. God chooses Abraham (Gen. 12), delivers Israel (Exodus 14), guides them to the promised land (Numbers), and gives them the instructions for blessing in the land (Deuteronomy).

In the Prophets, on the other hand, there is a *forward view* in expectation for the Messiah, whom they looked to by way of preparation and prophecy. The Prophets built upon the Mosaic foundation of the Law a house of Messianic hope from the rooftop of which they could look to the future fulfillment in Christ.

Poetry (Writings) adds a third direction—the *upward view* in aspiration for Christ. Much of what the poets wrote is not directly applicable to Christ, but beneath it all can be seen a longing look upward, an aspiration to something higher which, as a matter of fact, was only fully realized in Christ. Job once cried out for someone who could mediate between God and man (Job 9:33); the New Testament says, "There is one mediator between God and men, the man Christ Jesus" (I Tim. 2:5). Solomon aspired for perfect love (Song of Solomon); Jesus provided it (John 15:13, cf. I John 4:17-18). The book of Proverbs aspired for wisdom (cf. Prov. 8), and Christ *is* the wisdom of God (I Cor. 1:30, cf. Col. 2:3).

The "preacher" of Ecclesiastes sought happiness and satisfaction; Christ said, "These things I have spoken to you, that my joy may be in you, and that your joy may be full" (John 15:11). And so it goes throughout the "Writings"; there is an *upward aspiration* for Christ which is often unconscious but always present and never fully realized in any other than in the One in whom my soul delights.

The Propagation and Interpretation of Christ. The New Testament also lends itself to a threefold division. In such a division, the *manifestation* of Christ is presented in the Gospels; the *interpretation* of Christ in the Epistles; and the book of Acts considered separately records the *propagation* of Christ. This is a natural way to divide the New Testament and has been practiced from earliest times.[8] Acts is a history of the apostolic church and as such is naturally in a different class from the Epistles, which were messages to the early churches (and individuals).

Jesus had limited His early ministry for the most part to His homeland and the Jewish people. He said to a Canaanite woman, "I was sent only to the lost sheep of the house of Israel" (Matt. 15:24). When the Greeks inquired about Jesus, He replied, "Unless a grain of wheat falls into the earth and dies, it remains alone; but if it dies, it bears much fruit" (John 12:24). By this Jesus indicated that His present ministry was to die but that the fruits of His death would one day be shared with the Greeks. This propagation of Christ was to be fulfilled after His resurrection when Jesus commanded His followers to "go therefore and make disciples of *all nations*" (Matt. 28:19). His last words before the ascension were: "You shall be my witnesses in Jerusalem and in all Judea and Samaria and *to the end of the earth*" (Acts 1:8).

The book of Acts is a record of the fulfillment of this command; it is the story of the propagation of Christ into all the world. First the message of Christ, according to His command, went out in Jerusalem (Acts 2—5), then into all Judea

[8]Cf. Eusebius, *Church History*, III, 25.

(chaps. 6–7), and then into Samaria (chap. 8), and finally into all the world (chaps. 10–28). Whereas the thrust of Acts is primarily historical, the Epistles, in contrast, are theological. That is, the threefold division of the New Testament indicates that the Christ who was during His life manifest to the Jews, and in Acts propagated into all the world, is in the Epistles interpreted for the believers.

An Eightfold Christocentric Structure of Scripture

Basis of an Eightfold Division

When the Hebrew Old Testament was translated into Greek (called Septuagint or LXX) at Alexandria, Egypt (third century, B.C. and later), there was apparently a re-arranging of books based on their subject matter. Likewise, Jerome's Latin Vulgate (A.D., fourth-fifth century) groups the books according to their subject as *Law* (Genesis-Deuteronomy), *History* (Joshua-Nehemiah), *Poetry* (Job-Song of Solomon), and *Prophecy* (Isaiah-Malachi). This is the order of the Protestant Old Testament today. The New Testament has from the earliest times fallen into the categories of *Four Gospels, Acts, Epistles,* and *Revelation,* which, in standing last, forms a kind of fourth class, namely, New Testament prophecy. So from the early centuries of the Christian church down to the present the whole Bible has fallen naturally into its present eightfold topical structure as shown on the accompanying chart.[9]

Fourfold Parallel Between Old and New Testaments

This eightfold structure of the Scriptures reveals some

---

[9]Of course, the Bible could be classified into seven sections in various ways. The important thing is not how the Bible is divided but how it is related. No matter what the structure, Christ must be the theme. The eightfold structure is not treated here because it is believed to be divinely intended but because it is commonly accepted. Consequently, as with any generalization, some of the particulars may not fit perfectly.

Sixfold Structure	Eightfold Structure
Law—Foundation for Christ	Law—Foundation for Christ
Prophets—Expectation of Christ	History—Preparation for Christ
Writings—Aspiration for Christ	Poets—Aspiration for Christ
	Prophets—Expectation of Christ
Gospels—Manifestation of Christ	Gospels—Manifestation of Christ
Acts—Propagation of Christ	Acts—Propagation of Christ
Epistles—Interpretation of Christ	Epistles—Interpretation of Christ
	Revelation—Consummation in Christ

interesting parallels between the two Testaments. Once the History books of the Old Testament are made a separate class, there emerges a four-directional view: In the Law there is a *downward* look as the foundation is laid for Christ; in History there is an *outward* movement as the Jewish nation begins to make preparation for Christ; in Poetry there is an *upward* look in aspiration for Christ; and in Prophecy there is a *forward* view in expectation of Christ.[10] In the Law, God is acting upon His people to lay the footing for what follows; in History, the nation becomes active and moves out to conquer the land and establish the dynasty from which Christ the King will come. Without these preparations for Christ, there would have been no fulfillment of their aspirations and expectations.

Now the fourfold structure of the New Testament forms

[10]These directions or movements are not to be viewed as exhaustive of all spiritual movements within their sections but merely suggestive of the overall movement of the section generally.

84

an interesting parallel to this four-directional movement in the Old Testament sections as follows:

O. T.	Law	History	Poetry	Prophecy
Direction	Downward	Outward	Upward	Forward
N. T.	Gospels	Acts	Epistles	Revelation

Parallel Between Law and Gospels. Both Law and Gospels have a downward movement. In the Law, God comes down to dwell in the world in *symbolic form* (tabernacles, Christophanies, etc.); in the Gospels, God dwells in the world in *human form* (John 1:14). In the Law, the foundation is laid so that the nation of Israel can be built upon it; in the Gospels, the cornerstone is laid for the church to be built on it (Eph. 2:20; Matt. 16:16-18). In the Law there is one central figure, Moses, who instructs the people in God's righteousness; in the Gospels, Christ, the central Figure, teaches His followers to seek God's righteousness (Matt. 6:33).

Although both Law and Gospels have a downward movement, and both are basic to the rest of their respective Testaments, and both have as their head one central teacher of righteousness, yet there are some basic differences too. There is, of course, the obvious difference summed up earlier in which the truth of the New Testament transcends the teaching of the Old Testament. Then there is the immeasurable difference between the central figures of each Testament, Christ and Moses. Hebrews summarizes this difference in these words: "Now Moses was faithful *in* all God's house as a *servant*, to testify to the things that were to be spoken later, but Christ was faithful *over* God's house as a *son*" (3:5-6). Both men were faithful to God's household, but Moses was only a servant in the house. Christ was a Son over the house. Moses was vindicated as God's servant when the earth opened and swallowed His enemies (Num. 16:32). Christ was upheld as God's Son when the heavens opened and the voice said, "This is my beloved Son, with whom I am well pleased; listen to him" (Matt. 17:5, cf. 3:17). And even Moses was there to listen, and rejoice, for he had written of Christ (John 5:46).

Parallel Between History and Acts. History in the Old Testament and Acts in the New Testament bear some important parallels as they relate to Christ. First, they both have an *outward* direction. In Joshua the Israelites move out in victory over the world; in Acts the churches likewise turn "the world upside down" (Acts 17:6). Israel has its dark days (Judges) and the church has its own difficulties (cf. Acts 5:1 ff.; 6:1 ff.), but both emerge victorious—Israel with the help of their prophets, priests and righteous kings (cf. Samuel-Chronicles) and the church with Christ who is their Prophet (Acts 3:22), Priest (7:55 ff.), and King (17:7). Then too, both sections record the history of their Testaments, and both see the people of God moving out in response to God's having moved upon them.

However, in this regard, Acts of the New Testament surpasses the History of the Old Testament to a very marked degree. Abram was told that he would become a great nation "through whom all the families of the earth shall be blessed" (Gen. 12:3, margin). This function, as a channel of Messianic blessing to the nations, was apparently not too well performed by the Jews of the Old Testament. There was an occasional Ruth or Rahab brought in and even a reluctant Jonah sent out, but by and large they failed to be the channel of blessing to their contemporary nations (cf. Rom. 11:7, 15, 21). Instead of sharing the blessings and promises of God, they hoarded them; instead of building bridges to the Gentiles, they constructed "the dividing wall of hostility" (Eph. 2:14). In Christ and His church, however, this wall was "broken down," and Jew and Gentile become "one new man" in Christ (2:15). So the church of the New Testament moves out into a wider circle than had the chosen nation of the Old Testament, until it at last will include men from every nation, tribe, people and tongue. The Old Testament History had merely moved out in preparation for Christ; the New Testament History (Acts) shows the church moving forward in the universal propagation of Christ.

Parallel Between Poetry and Epistles. In both Poetry and Epistles there is an upward look. The poets looked up in aspiration for a Prophet and King who could fulfill the longings of their hearts. The New Testament Epistles look up to Christ, their High Priest, who supplies the needs of their lives (cf. Heb. 4:14-16). In addition to this, both Poetry and Epistles are interpretations of the foundational truths which come before them. Poetry added nothing to the basic truth of the great acts and words of God recorded in the Law of Moses; rather, it was an interpretation and application of them (cf. Ps. 44, 89). For example, the great poetical book of Psalms is divided into five sections patterned after the fivefold division of the Law. Solomon's wisdom is but an interpretation and application of Moses' commandments.

In parallel to this, the Epistles are an interpretation of the great words and deeds of Christ recorded in the Gospels. The truth of the apostles is all based on the teaching of Christ.[11] Their doctrine is founded on Christ's deeds and words. It is true that both Poetry and Epistles explicate what Moses and Christ implied, but neither New Testament apostles nor Old Testament prophets explain what their forerunners did not somewhere foretell.

Both Poetry and Epistles hang their hopes on high: Poetry looking up in aspiration to Him who has not yet come, and the Epistles looking up to Him who has just departed and now ever lives on high to make intercessions for them (Heb. 7:25).

Parallel Between Prophets and Revelation. The prophets of the Old Testament and the book of Revelation in the New

[11]Even the truth of the mysterious union of Jew and Gentile in one body (Eph. 3:6) was taught by Christ to Paul (v. 3, cf. Gal. 1:12), to Peter (Acts 10:15), and may even be implied in the Gospels (Mark 7:19).

Testament sustain an obvious relationship: both are prophetic of Christ. Both look forward to the coming of Christ: the Old Testament to His first and second comings, and the New Testament only to Christ's second coming (Rev. 1:7; 22:12). That both Testaments should end with this same expectation is entirely appropriate, but there are also some essential differences. For one thing, the Old Testament Prophet Daniel was told, "Go your way . . . for the words are shut up and sealed until the time of the end" (Dan. 12:9). John, on the other hand, was told, "*Do not seal up the words of the prophecy of this book, for the time is near*" (Rev. 22:10). The Old Testament prophets looked forward in expectation for the day Christ would unseal the scroll of prophecy. Revelation in the New Testament looks forward to the *consummation* of all things in Christ, who is about to unloose the seals of prophecy. At best the Old Testament prophets attained here and there to revelations of the coming Christ; John received "*the* revelation of Jesus Christ" (Rev. 1:1).

In all the enigma that surrounds the interpretation of the book of Revelation, there is perhaps only one really fatal mistake—the failure to see that the book is not a prophetic puzzle to be put together by the clever interpreter; it is the revelation of *Jesus Christ*. It tells us that He for whom Moses laid the foundation, He for whom the history of Israel made preparation, He to whom the poets and prophets looked in aspiration and expectation, and He whose manifestation is in the Gospels, propagation and interpretation in Acts and the Epistles, will be the final goal and *consummation* of all things as well.

5

CHRIST IN EACH BOOK OF THE BIBLE

This chapter is a culmination of all that has preceded it. First, Christ was presented as the key to the inspiration and interpretation of the whole Bible (chap. 1). From this there followed an attempt to determine the various ways in which Christ is the theme of the Old Testament (chap. 2). Then Christ was presented as the tie between the two Testaments, relating one to the other as anticipation is related to realization (chap. 3). In the last chapter (chap. 4), Christ was related to the various ways of dividing the Bible into sections. In this chapter Christ will be presented as the underlying theme of every book of the Bible. Of course it would be going too far to suggest that Christ is the explicit or dominant theme of each individual book in the Bible, for this is apparently not so.[1] However, in the light of Jesus' clear claims—as explained in the foregoing chapters—one would not be going far enough unless Christ is seen as the implicit or underlying theme of all of Scripture. Sometimes this Christocentric theme is one with the main theme of a book and sometimes not, but it is always there. That is, each individual book in the Scriptures contributes some threads of truth to the overall fabric. Since the Bible as a whole speaks of Christ, then all the parts must somehow contribute to that whole.

[1]Some books have an obvious historical theme (as Ezra or Esther) or a personal theme (as Philemon) or a moral theme (as many prophets) that only an unwarranted spiritualization could misconstrue as *primarily* Christocentric.

The Law: The Foundation for Christ

Following the eightfold division of our present-day Bible, the four sections of the Old Testament view Christ in anticipation, and the four New Testament divisions present Christ in realization. Christ may be seen in the Old Testament by way of anticipation in four basic ways: (1) The Law laid *the foundation* for Christ's coming; (2) History made *preparation* for it; (3) Poetry looked up in *aspiration* to it; (4) Prophets looked forward in *expectation* for it.

Now the books of the Law laid the foundation for Christ in that they recorded the preparation of a Messianic nation through whom Christ would come and over whom He would reign as King. God's plan was to bless "all the families of the earth" (Gen. 12:3), but He chose one nation through which He would accomplish this purpose. So, in the overall sense of the word, Christ is the theme of the entire Old Testament only indirectly, by way of the preparation of the nation which would produce the Messiah. Of course, Christ is in the Old Testament in more ways than by way of overall preparation. He is there also by way of prophecy and prefigurations (types, etc., cf. chap. 2). Here, however, the concern is primarily with overall preparation for Christ in the Old Testament, as viewed through a fourfold structure.

GENESIS: THE ELECTION OF THE NATION

The first step in the preparation for Christ was the choice of the nation which would be the channel through which Christ would come. Chapters 1-11 of Genesis present a brief sketch of the creation (chaps. 1-2), and corruption of the *nations* (chaps. 3-6) with the resultant cataclysm of the flood (chaps. 7-9). Following this, the divine curse fell on the Cainite civilization at Babel (chaps. 10-11). In the last chapters of Genesis (chaps. 12-50), God turned from the nations in general to the *chosen nation* in particular. This nation began with Abraham (chaps. 12-24), continued in his son Isaac (chaps. 25-27), and in Isaac's son, Jacob (chaps 28-36).

These people were miraculously preserved by Joseph (chaps. 37-50), and, in God's providence, Jacob's whole family descended into Egypt.

EXODUS: THE REDEMPTION OF THE NATION

God's perfect will was for the chosen nation to remain in the promised land and to "not go down to Egypt" (Gen. 26:2). However, in God's permissive will, He told Jacob: "Do not be afraid to go down to Egypt" (Gen. 46:3), so that in His providential will and by a redemptive act, God could say, "I loved him, and out of Egypt I called my son" (Hosea 11:1). The first part of Exodus recorded the *redemption* of the nation (chaps. 1-18), and the last part recorded the *revelation* for the nation (chaps. 19-40) in the tables of the law (chaps. 19-24), teaching obedience, and in the tabernacle (chaps. 25-40), teaching worship.[2]

LEVITICUS: THE SANCTIFICATION OF THE NATION

"You shall be holy; for I the LORD your God am holy" (19:2) is the key thought throughout the book. In Genesis, Israel was chosen to righteousness; in Exodus, they were declared righteous by redemption; and in Leviticus, God desired to make them righteous by sanctification. In Exodus they were brought into union with God; in Leviticus they were led unto communion with Him. Exodus shows their pardon and Leviticus their purity or holiness. The first part of Leviticus reveals that the *way* to the holy One (chaps. 1-10) is by oblation (sacrifice) and mediation (priesthood). The last part teaches that the *walk* of holiness (chaps. 11-27) is by separation (purity of body) and sanctification (purity of soul).

NUMBERS: THE DIRECTION TO THE NATION

Whereas Leviticus called the nation to worship God, Numbers called them to walk with God. The directions from the

[2]Many of the basic outline forms used here are adapted from W. G. Scroggie, *Know Your Bible* (New York: Revell, 1940).

Lord were clear (chaps. 1-10), "Go in and possess the land."
The disbelief in the Lord was just as marked (chaps. 11-14).
They were *discontent* with God's provision (chaps. 11-12)
and *disbelieved* His promises (chaps. 13-14). Consequently
the people received *discipline* from the Lord (chaps. 15-36).
For forty years they wandered, murmured and were numbered until all the older generation passed away (chaps.
15-26), and the new generation had been prepared (chaps.
27-36) to enter into the land. The dead bodies of the disobedient filled the mortuary of Numbers, as the souls of the
obedient had filled the sanctuary of Leviticus.

DEUTERONOMY: THE INSTRUCTION FOR THE NATION

Before the elected nation could become a victorious nation,
they had to be an instructed nation. Whereas Genesis recorded the ruin of man, Exodus the redemption of Israel,
Leviticus their religion, and Numbers their rebellion, Deuteronomy gave the regulations to Israel which were necessary
for them to enter their rest in Joshua. In these great fare-
well speeches of Deuteronomy, Moses looked in *retrospect*
at their historical life (chaps. 1-4), in *introspect* at their
legal life (chaps. 5-26), and in *prospect* to their prophetical
life (chaps. 27-34).

These five books of the Law laid the foundation for Christ
not only *nationally*, as they unfolded in the history of the
nation which was to give birth to the Messiah, but also *theologically*, in that Christ is the Elector (Genesis), Redeemer
(Exodus), Sanctifier (Leviticus), Guide (Numbers), and
Teacher (Deuteronomy).

HISTORY: THE PREPARATION FOR CHRIST

In the Law, God acted upon the nation. In History that
nation begins to act for God. Moses had brought Israel out
of *bondage* but then Joshua led them into *blessing*. Moses
gave them their law, Joshua gave them their land. The
foundation was laid in the Law, and here preparation is
made for Christ in the history of Israel.

JOSHUA: THE POSSESSION OF THE NATION

After the death of Moses, God told Joshua, "Arise, go over this Jordan, . . . into the land which I am giving to them, to the people of Israel" (Joshua 1:2). Immediately they *entered* the land (1:1–5:12), *conquered* the land (5:13– 12:24), *possessed* the land (chaps. 13-25). "So Joshua took the whole land, according to all that the LORD had spoken to Moses; and Joshua gave it for an inheritance to Israel" (11:23).

JUDGES: THE OPPRESSION OF THE NATION

The book of Judges shifted the scene from victory to apostasy. The nation had at first overtaken the nations of the land, but subsequently it was overtaken by these same nations. Israel turned from faithfulness to faithlessness. While the nation met with a temporary setback in its preparation for Christ, it manifested at the same time a more vivid need for the Saviour-Statesman. The *reason* judges were needed was because of Israel's apostasy (1:1–3:8). The *rule* of the judges was one of sporatic loyalty (3:9– 16:31), and the final *ruin* of the judges came by national anarchy (chaps. 19-21), when "every man did what was right in his own eyes" (21:25). In all, the nation passed through seven cycles, each including sin, servitude, supplication and salvation (cf. 2:16 ff.).

RUTH: THE DEVOTION WITHIN THE NATION

A notable exception to the impurity of the time of the judges is the purity of Ruth. The book stands out as a lily in the muddy background of the judges. It is a story of devotion in a day of declension, of faithfulness in a time of unfaithfulness. Ruth became the ancestor of David (4:22) through whom the Messiah was to come.

I SAMUEL: THE STABILIZATION OF THE NATION

The unsettled condition and anarchy of the judges gave

way to the stability of the monarchy of Saul. It was *Samuel's* judgeship (chaps. 1-7) that provided the connecting link between the judges and *Saul's* kingship (chaps. 8-15). But the people, with wrong motives, had clamored for a king (I Sam. 8:5), and their choice of a king was from the wrong tribe (Benjamin rather than Judah). As a result, Saul, the people's choice, had to give way to *David*, God's choice (chaps. 16-31). Under David they received the monarch God wanted (13:14).

II SAMUEL: THE EXPANSION OF THE NATION

During the reigns of David (II Samuel) and Solomon (I Kings 1-10), Israel's borders were extended and her temple built. David's *fame* was shown by his recognition on the throne (chaps. 1-10). However, his *shame* led to his rejection from the throne (chaps. 11-18), but finally the *name* of David was preserved by his restoration to the throne (chaps. 19-24). The foundation had been laid for Christ in the Law, but here in History the preparation was made for Christ, who was to come as the Son of David and to reign in Jerusalem (II Sam. 7:12 ff.).

I KINGS: THE DETERIORATION OF THE NATION

In the first verse of I Kings 11 these ominous words occur, "Now King Solomon loved many foreign women." From this juncture the deterioration of the kingdom became apparent. The united monarchy of Solomon (chaps. 1-11) gave way to the divided monarchies of Israel and Judah (chaps. 12-22). At Solomon's death his captain, Jeroboam, revolted with the ten northern tribes called Israel, while his son Rehoboam became king over the southern tribes of Judah and Benjamin which were called Judah.

II KINGS: THE DEPORTATION OF THE NATION

There were three basic reasons why Israel fell to the Assyrians in 722 B.C. and Judah fell to the Babylonians in 586 B.C.

1. Religiously, there was idolatry (cf. I Kings 11:4; 12:28-29).
2. Morally, immorality was commonplace (I Kings 11:1-11; 14:24).
3. Politically, disunity had divided the nation in two (I Kings 12:16-19).

The record of the decline and deportation of *Israel* (chaps. 1-17) contains not even one good king. In the decline and deportation of *Judah* (chaps. 18-25) there are only a few notable exceptions to this bleak picture of unrighteous royalty. But these exceptions could not permanently resist the tidal wave of evil, and even Judah was carried into captivity for seventy years (II Kings 24:2), just as Jeremiah the prophet had predicted (25:11).

I AND II CHRONICLES: THE HISTORY OF THE NATION REPEATED

Kings is primarily political history, while Chronicles is religious history. Kings is written from the prophetic point of view, and Chronicles from the priestly. First Chronicles parallels I and II Samuel, and II Chronicles parallels I and II Kings, although Chronicles deals only with Judah.

ESTHER: THE PRESERVATION OF THE NATION

It would appear as if God's Messianic purpose for the nation was lost with the conquest and captivity of Judah by the Babylonians, but this was not so. The nation was deported but not destroyed. Despite the grave dangers at the hands of Haman the Persian (chaps. 1-4), they received a great deliverance through Esther (chaps. 5-10). And even though the name of God is absent from this book, the hand of God is evident in the preservation of His people. Preparation for the Messiah was continued by way of the preservation of the Messianic nation (cf. 4:14).

EZRA: THE RESTORATION OF THE NATION

In spite of the fact that the nation had declined and was

deported, it was nevertheless protected by God so that the people could be returned and restored to their land. God stirred the heart of Cyrus the king in 539 B.C. and almost 50,000 Jews returned under *Zerubbabel* (chaps. 1-6). Later, in 458 B.C., about 2,000 more returned under *Ezra* (chaps. 7-10), as the people were repatriated.

NEHEMIAH: THE RECONSTRUCTION OF THE NATION

In Ezra, Judah rebuilt its religious life (temple), but in Nehemiah its political life was rebuilt. This reconstruction involved not only the *rebuilding* of the city (chaps. 1-7), but also the *revival* of the citizens (chaps. 8-13). Everything was restored except the king. Over four hundred "silent years" passed before "the time had fully come" (Gal. 4:4) for Christ to appear and for men to ask, "Where is he who has been born king of the Jews?" (Matt. 2:2).

POETRY: ASPIRATION FOR CHRIST

The Law has a downward view to the foundation for Christ, the History has an outward view in preparation for Christ, but Poetry has an upward view in aspiration for Christ. Whereas the Law deals with Israel's moral life, and the History reveals her national life, the poetical books are concerned with her spiritual or practical life.

JOB: ASPIRATION FOR MEDIATION BY CHRIST

Job desired someone who "would maintain the right of a man with God" (16:21). His longing was for someone to be a mediator "who might lay his hand upon both" God and man (9:33). He asked if there was any significance to suffering, any purpose to pain, or any meaning to human misery. What Job did not recognize in the depth of his despair was that whatever happens *on the scene* (chaps. 3-41) can only be fully understood in the light of what takes place *behind the scene* (chaps. 1-2), where the accuser of the brethren accuses them day and night before God, and in view of what will be their reward *beyond the scene* (chap. 42). Furthermore, what Job desired, without fully understanding, was the Advocate (I John 2:1) or High Priest who could "sympathize with our weaknesses" (Heb. 4:15). He did not realize that the significance of suffering was to be found in the substitution of the Saviour who suffered "the righteous for the unrighteous, that he might bring us to God" (I Peter 3:18). In short, what Job really desired was the "one mediator between God and men, the man Christ Jesus" (I Tim. 2:5).

PSALMS: ASPIRATION FOR COMMUNION WITH CHRIST

Whereas Job debates the "why" of calamity, Psalms emphasizes the "how" of piety. Prayer and praise, the divine language of the soul, fill the pages of Psalms. This communion with God relates not only to His *creation* (Ps. 1-41), but to His *redemption* (Ps. 42-72), to His *sanctuary* (Ps. 73-89), to His *providence* (Ps. 90-106), and to His *ethics* as well (Ps. 107-50). At times this implicit aspiration for communion with Christ in Psalms buds into an explicit Messianic communication about Christ (cf. Ps. 22). However, the aspirations of the psalms are not brought into fruition until, through the condescension, crucifixion, resurrection and intercession of Christ, the way of access is opened that men may "with confidence draw near to the throne of grace" (Heb. 4:16).

PROVERBS: ASPIRATION FOR WISDOM IN CHRIST

This wisdom was "practical prudence" or a sort of "sanctified sense" that enabled believers not only to apprehend truth in their minds but to apply truth to their lives. The aspiration in Proverbs is for wisdom to become incarnate (Prov. 8), as indeed it did when "all the treasures of wisdom and knowledge" became flesh in Christ (Col. 2:3). So in Proverbs the aspiration is for wisdom as reflected in words *to* the wise (chaps. 1-9), *of* the wise (10:1—22:16), *for* the wise (22:17—24:34), and *from* the wise (chaps. 25-31). But what the Old Testament saints aspired to in precept, the New Testament saints had in person, as Christ Himself is "made . . . [unto them] wisdom" (I Cor. 1:30).

ECCLESIASTES: ASPIRATION FOR SATISFACTION IN CHRIST

The philosophers have always speculated on the nature of the "greatest good" (*summum bonum*). When the wise teacher of Ecclesiastes set out in quest for it, he sought it first *experientially* (chaps. 1-2), by trying wine, women and works. He discovered, however, that all this was but vanity and vexation of spirit. He then studied the issue *philosophically* (chaps. 3-12), by means of wealth and wisdom, only to arrive at the same conclusion: there is no happiness "under the sun." He learned that happiness must be found beyond the sun, in the Son, as he writes, "Fear God, and keep his commandments; for this is the whole duty of man" (12:13), saying that these words are "given by one Shepherd" (12:11). Thus, his aspiration is to the Good Shepherd (John 10), and for the greatest good, which in the New Testament is found in "the prize of the upward call of God in Christ Jesus" (Phil. 3:14).

SONG OF SOLOMON: ASPIRATION FOR UNION WITH CHRIST

Literally, this canticle speaks of the intimate marital union. Spiritually, however, the Song of Solomon pictures the relationship between Israel and Jehovah, or between God and the individual.[3] There is a growing maturity in the union of love which progresses from possession of the Beloved (2:16) to being possessed by the Beloved (6:3), to the full realization of the passion of the Beloved for His bride (7:10). The canticler is aspiring to that intimacy shared in the mystery of Christ's love for and union with His beloved bride (Eph. 5:32).

[3]And, it might be added, figuratively the Song of Solomon pictures Christ's love for His bride, the church (cf. Eph. 5:25, 32).

98

PROPHECY: EXPECTATION OF CHRIST

The foundation for Christ was firmly laid in the Law, preparation was providentially made in History, and aspiration was spiritually expressed in Poetry. In the books of Prophecy this aspiration came to fruition in the Messianic expectation of Christ. Whereas the Law looked downward to the foundation, History looked outward in preparation, Poetry looked upward in aspiration, the prophetical books looked forward in expectation. The Law gave the moral aspect of the people, History the national, Poetry the spiritual, and Prophecy gave the prophetical aspect.

The seventeen prophetical books fall into three classes: the preexilic prophets (Isaiah, Jeremiah, Hosea through Zephaniah) whose *admonitions* were uttered before the final fall of Jerusalem (586 B.C.), the exilic books (Lamentations, Ezekiel, Daniel) whose *anticipation* during the seventy-year captivity was for restoration to their land, and the postexilic prophets (Haggai, Zechariah, Malachi), whose *exhortation* to the repatriated remnant was to rebuild the fallen nation. All of these prophets share the expectation of Christ, but each does so in his own way.

ISAIAH

Isaiah had many Messianic expectations. He foresaw Christ as the Lord "high and lifted up" (6:1), the Son of a virgin (7:14), the "Mighty God" and "Prince of Peace" (9:6), a smitten Lamb (chap. 53), the Anointed (Messiah) of the Lord (61:1 ff.), but above all, Christ is seen as the suffering Servant (cf. chaps. 53-62).

JEREMIAH

Jeremiah pictures Christ as "the fountain of living waters" (2:13), the "balm in Gilead" (8:22), the good Shepherd (23:4), as David the King (30:9), "a righteous Branch" (23:5), and as "The LORD our righteousness" (23:6).

LAMENTATIONS

Lamentations provides prophetic pictures of Christ as the Afflicted of the Lord (1:12), despised of His enemies (2:15-16), "laughingstock of all peoples" (3:14), smitten and insulted One (3:30), but behind them all is Christ the weeping Prophet (cf. Matt. 23:37 ff.).

EZEKIEL

Ezekiel anticipates Christ, the Restorer of the nation (chap. 37), the Shepherd of the flock (34:23), Cleanser of the nation (36:24 ff.), but above all he sees Christ as the Glory of God (cf. chaps. 1, 43).

DANIEL

Daniel foretells Christ as the "stone . . . cut from a mountain by no human hand" (2:45), the "anointed one [Messiah]" (9:26), the "Son of man" (7:13), and the "Ancient of Days" (7:22).

HOSEA

Hosea sees Christ as the only Saviour (13:4), the Son of God (11:1), the One who ransoms from the dead (13:14), but primarily as the compassionate Lover (11:4).

JOEL

Joel predicted that Christ would pour out His Spirit (2:28), judge the nations (3:2, 12), and would be the "refuge to his people, a stronghold to the people of Israel" (3:16).

AMOS

Amos pictures Christ as "an only son" (8:10), the One who will rebuild the "tabernacle of David" (9:11, ASV), and He who is the Husbandman of His people (9:13).

OBADIAH

Obadiah portrays Christ as the Lord of the kingdom (v. 21), and Deliverer of the holy remnant (v. 17).

JONAH

Jonah pictures Christ as the Prophet to the nations (3:4), and the resurrected One (1:17, cf. Matt. 12:40).

MICAH

Micah predicted Christ as the "God of Jacob" (4:2), the Judge of the nations (4:3) and the "ruler in Israel" (5:2).

NAHUM

Nahum sees Christ as the "jealous God" (1:2), the Avenger of His adversaries.

HABAKKUK

Habakkuk pictured Christ as the "Holy One" (1:12), who justifies the righteous by faith (2:4), and who will one day fill the earth "with the knowledge . . . of the LORD" (2:14).

ZEPHANIAH

Zephaniah views Christ as the righteous Lord within Israel (3:5), the witness against the nations (3:8), and the King of Israel, the LORD (3:15).

HAGGAI

Haggai sees Christ as the Restorer of the temple's glory (1:7-9), the Overthrower of kingdoms (2:22), and the "signet ring" to Israel (2:23).

ZECHARIAH

Zechariah is filled with Messianic expectations. He views Christ as God's "servant the Branch" (3:8), the triumphant King (9:9), the Shepherd of the doomed (11:7), "him whom they have pierced" (12:10), fountain of cleansing (13:1), "king over all the earth" (14:9), and "the King, the LORD of hosts" (14:17).

MALACHI

Malachi expects Christ to return to His temple as "the

messenger of the covenant" (3:1), "like a refiner's fire" (3:2), and as *"the sun of righteousness"* arising with healing in His wings (4:2).

Each prophet had his own set of Messianic metaphors, but all shared the common Messianic hope. Theirs was the expectation of the Christ for whom Moses laid the foundation, for whom the nation had made preparation, and to whom the poets had looked in aspiration.

The Gospels: The Manifestation of Christ

The anticipation of the Old Testament is the realization of the New Testament. The Old Testament deals with the national preparation and expectation of Christ; the Gospels provided the personal *manifestation* of the Saviour. His manifestation as recorded in the Gospels is fourfold. The accompanying chart illustrates this manifestation of Christ, under its many metaphors.

CHRIST IN THE FOUR GOSPELS

Book	Matthew	Mark	Luke	John
Theme	King (Zech. 9:9)	Servant (Isa. 52:13)	Man (Zech. 6:12)	God (Isa. 40:10)
Presented	To Jews	To Romans	To Greeks	To World
Ancestry	To Abraham and David	None	Adam	God
Traced	To Royalty	(Anonymity)	To Humanity (Adam)	To Eternity
Symbol	Lion (Ezek. 1:10)	Ox	Man	Eagle
Emphasis	What He Taught	What He Wrought	What He Sought	What He Thought
Provision	Righteousness (3:15)	Service (10:45)	Redemption (19:10)	Life (10:10)
Key Word	Sovereignty	Ministry	Humanity	Deity
Pictured as	Promised Saviour	Powerful Saviour	Perfect Saviour	Personal Saviour

MATTHEW: CHRIST IS MANIFEST AS ROYALTY

His lineage is traced to a sovereign (the Son of David) and to a sacrifice (the Son of Abraham) (Matt. 1:1). Christ is represented by the symbol of the lion Ezek. 1:10), the king of beasts. In the words of Zechariah, the Jews are told, "Lo, your *king* comes to you" (9:9).

MARK: CHRIST IS MANIFEST IN HIS MINISTRY

He is the Servant of Jehovah (Isa. 53:11), symbolized by the ox, and presented to the Romans. His ancestry is not traced (a servant needs none), but His activity is predominant. Matthew stressed what Jesus taught, but Mark emphasized what Jesus wrought (Mark 10:45), as Isaiah said, "Behold, my servant" (Isa. 52:13).

LUKE: CHRIST IS MANIFEST IN HIS PERFECT HUMANITY

Christ's ancestry is here traced to the first man, Adam. Luke stressed not what Jesus taught (as Matthew did) or wrought (as Mark did), but what He sought. Luke writes, "For the son of man came to seek and to save the lost" (19:10). Zechariah stated the theme in advance when he wrote, "Behold, the man" (6:12).

JOHN: CHRIST IS MANIFEST IN HIS DEITY

John writes, "In the beginning was the Word, and the Word was with God, and the Word was God," and "the Word became flesh and dwelt among us" (John 1:1, 14). He does not trace Christ's ancestry to human royalty (as Matthew did), or leave it in anonymity (as Mark did), nor trace it to the origin of humanity (as Luke did), but he traces it to deity and to eternity. In John, Christ is seen as the eagle soaring into the heavens and, as in no other gospel, it is manifest what Jesus thought (cf. John 13-17). In Matthew, Jesus fulfills man's needs for righteousness (cf. 3:15); in Mark, man's need for service (10:45); in Luke, man's need of redemption (19:10); and in John, man's need for life (10:10).

Thus, the four Gospels record the historical manifestation of Christ, not for a sectarian segment of society, nor merely for a religious remnant, but for the Jews, for the Greeks, and for the Romans; yes, for the whole world. But Jesus was in the world and "the world knew him not. He came unto his own home, and his own people received him not" (John 1:10-11). The revelation of Christ was for all, but the reception of Christ was by the few who believed (1:12).

ACTS: THE EVANGELIZATION OR PROPAGATION OF CHRIST

In Acts the scene shifts from the historical manifestation of Christ to the world evangelization of Christ. Jesus had limited His own earthly ministry mostly to Israel, but He had conmmanded His disciples to take the message to the nations (Matt. 28:19; Acts 1:8). As far back as Genesis 12, when preparation was made for Christ by the selection of Abraham, the stated purpose of God was that "all the families of the earth" would be blessed. The realization of that promise is recorded in the propagation of the message of Christ by the apostles in Acts.

The key to Acts is in Christ's command to His followers to be His witnesses "in Jerusalem and in all Judea and Samaria and to the end of the earth" (1:8). As a result of the out-pouring of the Spirit, the message of Christ went into Jerusalem (chaps. 1-6); as a result of the overwhelming persecution, the gospel entered all Judea (chap. 7), and Samaria (chap. 8); and as a result of Paul's conversion and missionary vision, Christ was propagated to the end of the earth (chaps. 9-28, cf. Col. 1:23).

THE EPISTLES: INTERPRETATION AND APPLICATION OF CHRIST

The Gospels and Acts record the manifestation and evangelization of Christ into all the world; the Pauline and General Epistles reveal the interpretation and application of Christ to the believers. This distinction helps explain the reason why the parabolic method of teaching is predominant in the Gospels and the didactic method is used in the Epistles. Jesus usually spoke in parables to the crowd so that truth not yet accepted might be put in terms already accepted by them. The Epistles, on the other hand, speak in direct terms to the disciples, who had already accepted the truth but needed further interpretation of it. So the parabolic method was more suitable for evangelization and illustration of the truth, and the didactic method yields more readily to the interpretation and application of the truth. It is this latter form which is used in the Epistles.

PAULINE EPISTLES: EXPOSITION OF CHRIST

The primary stress in Paul's epistles is the exposition or interpretation of Christ to the believers, which necessarily involved application as well. In the General Epistles, the primary emphasis is on the exhortation to the things of Christ or, in other words, the application of Christ to the believers, which necessarily involved some interpretation as well.

Paul always places the key at the "front door" of his epistles, for their themes are generally stated as those "possessions" which the believer is said to have "in Christ."[4]

Romans: Redemption in Christ. This book is the great exposition of the believer's *"redemption* which is in Christ Jesus" (3:24). It is a declaration of the righteousness of God (1:17), reckoned to men through faith in Jesus Christ (cf. 4:5).

I Corinthians: Sanctification in Christ. The book is addressed "to those *sanctified* in Christ Jesus, called to be saints" (1:2). Whereas Romans revealed how God could *declare* a man righteous (cf. Rom. 3:21-26), I Corinthians shows that it is necessary to *make* a man righteous as well. The first is the act of justification, and the second is the process of sanctification.

---

[4]Usually this phrase occurs in the first chapter of the epistle, and it is most often the first reference to "in Christ" that provides the theme of the epistle. This procedure is quite clear in Romans through II Thessalonians. A comparison of this chapter with the work of W. G. Scroggie, *Christ the Key to Scripture* (Chicago: Bible Inst. Colportage Assn., 1924), will reveal some close parallels, although the material is developed differently.

II Corinthians: Jubilation in Christ. For those, as Paul, who attempt to live the life of sanctification which will necessarily involve perils and persecutions (II Tim. 3:12, cf. II Cor. 11:23 ff.), there will be the expression of *jubilation* (triumph) in Christ. "But thanks be to God, who *in Christ* leads us in triumph . . ." (2:14). The believer has triumphant victory in his ministry (cf. I Cor. 4).

Galatians: Emancipation in Christ. Galatians was written as a warning about those "who slipped in to spy out our *freedom* which we have in Christ Jesus, that they might bring us into bondage" (2:4). It is the Christians' emancipation proclamation. Paul urges the believers: "For *freedom* Christ set us free; stand fast therefore, and do not submit again to a yoke of slavery" (5:1).

Ephesians: Exaltation and Unification in Christ. This letter is addressed to those blessed "in Christ with every spiritual blessing in the *heavenly places*" (1:3). However, there are several converging themes "in Christ." The believer has this exaltation in Christ only because he has election in Christ (1:4), the result of which is union or *unification* in Christ (1:10). Around this latter point of unity, most of the epistle seems to revolve (cf. 2:14; 4:3 ff.).

Philippians: Exultation (Joy) in Christ. According to this letter, Paul desired that the believers "may have ample cause to *glory* [exult] in Christ Jesus" (1:26). Despite the fact that the apostle was imprisoned, he said, "I am glad and *rejoice* with you all. Likewise you also should be glad and *rejoice* with me" (2:17-18; cf. 1:18). "*Rejoice* in the Lord always; again I will say, *Rejoice*" (4:4), and, "Finally, my brethren, *rejoice in the* Lord" (3:1); all of these are part of Paul's continual *exultation* in Christ Jesus.

Colossians: Completion in Christ. In this book Paul is "warning every man and teaching every man in all wisdom, that we may present every man *mature* [complete, perfect] *in Christ*" (1:28). They are warned against any philosophy that would deny the *"fulness"* of Christ's deity (2:9) so that they may "come to *fulness* of life in him" (2:10). Paul prays that they "may stand *mature* [complete] and *fully* assured in all the will of God" (4:12). Nothing can be added to Christ's deity or ministry, and we are complete in Him.

I Thessalonians: Expectation in Christ. The apostle begins his letter by thanking God for the Thessalonians' "work of faith and labor of love and steadfastness of *hope in our Lord Jesus Christ*" (1:3). The stress is on the latter, since Christ's coming is mentioned in every chapter (1:10; 2:19; 3:13; 4:16; 5:23). Now since "hope" in the New Testament means to have confidence in what is coming (Heb. 6:11) and not a mere desire or wish, then it is *expectation* in Christ that Paul expresses here.

II Thessalonians: Glorification in Christ. When the expectation of Christ has become a realization at His coming, then, says Paul to the Thessalonians, "the name of our Lord Jesus may be *glorified* in you, and you [*glorified*] *in him*" (1:12). The saints will be glorified in Him "when he comes . . . to be *glorified* in his saints" (1:10).

I Timothy: Faithfulness in Christ. Timothy is reminded of "the faith and love that are in Christ Jesus" (1:14) and to keep on "holding *faith* and a good conscience" (1:19). Paul said he thanked God, "because he judged me *faithful* by appointing me to his service" (1:12). Timothy was urged to "fight the good fight of the *faith*" (6:12) and to "hold the mystery of the *faith*" (3:9). It was a day of apostasy (4:1 ff.), which demanded faithfulness in the servants of Christ (cf. 3:11).

II Timothy: Soundness in Christ. In II Timothy he is urged to maintain *soundness* in Christ. "Follow the pattern of the *sound words* which you have heard from me, in the faith and love which are *in Christ Jesus*" (1:13). "For the time is coming when people will not endure *sound* teaching" (4:3).

Titus: Steadfastness in Christ. Like Timothy, Titus is

urged "to give instruction in *sound doctrine*" (1:9, cf. 2:1) and to be "*sound* in faith" (2:2) and told to "declare these things; exhort and reprove with all authority" (2:15), or, in other words, "he must hold firm to the sure word" (1:9); he must be *steadfast* in the faith.

Philemon: Benefaction in Christ. The conversion of this runaway slave provides an excellent illustration of "all the *good* that is ours *in Christ*" (v. 6). Again, Paul says, "That your *goodness* might not be of compulsion" (v. 14). This goodness or these *benefits* in Christ included the material and social as well as the spiritual dimensions of the gospel.

GENERAL EPISTLES: EXHORTATION IN CHRIST

Paul's epistles, particularly the first ten, are predominantly an exposition and interpretation of Christ; the General Epistles are primarily an application of Christ or an exhortation about Christ, although they contain expositions as well. These epistles also differ from Paul's in that his were usually direct to a given church or individual, whereas the General Epistles had a wider audience (cf. James 1:1; I Peter 1:1).

Hebrews: Exhortation to Perfection. The writer exhorted the Hebrews, saying, "Wherefore leaving the doctrine of the first principles of Christ, let us press on unto *perfection*" (6:1, ASV). Christ was "better than" everything the Old Testament could offer (1:4; 7:19, 22; 8:6, etc.). The Old Testament sacrifices "cannot *perfect* the conscience" (9:9) but Christ, "through the greater and more *perfect* tabernacle" (9:11, margin), and "by a single offering . . . has *perfected* for all time those who are sanctified" (10:14). Since Christ supersedes the Old Testament, there are very strong warnings to those who do not press on to the perfection in Christ (cf. 2:1-4; 10:26; 12:15).

James: Exhortation to Wisdom in Christ. "If any of you lacks *wisdom*, let him ask God" (1:5), James urged. "Who is *wise* and understanding among you? By his good life let him show his *works* in the meekness of *wisdom*" (3:13). So "works" follow upon wisdom, and this "*wisdom* from above is first pure, then peaceable, gentle, open to reason, full of mercy and good fruits" (3:17).

I Peter: Exhortation to Submission. Peter addresses the letter to those who were "sanctified by the Spirit for *obedience to Jesus Christ*" (1:2). Throughout the book there is an exhortation to submission (2:13, 18; 5:5) and obedience (1:14, 22), and especially to patient suffering. "But if when you do right and suffer for it you take it patiently, you have God's approval" (2:20).

II Peter: Exhortation to Purification in Christ. The book is written "to those who have obtained a faith . . . in the *righteousness* of our God and Savior Jesus Christ" (1:1), who has granted "all things that pertain to life and *godliness*, through the knowledge of [Christ]" (1:3, cf. 3:11). All of this godliness and *purification* is by way of an education ("knowledge," 1:2, 5, 6, 8, etc.), that is, by a growth "in the grace and knowledge of our Lord and Savior Jesus Christ" (3:18).

I John: Exhortation to Communion with Christ. John urges the believers: "If we walk in the light, as he [Christ] is in the light, we have *fellowship* with one another " (1:7). The fellowship or *communion* is in the light (chaps. 1-2) and in love (chaps. 3-4), but it is *with God* and Christ. "Our *fellowship* is with the Father and with his Son Jesus Christ" (1:3).

II John: Exhortation for a Continuation in Christ. "I rejoiced greatly to find some of your children *following* the truth" (4). "*Look to yourselves*, that you may not lose what you have worked for" (8). He speaks of *abiding* (9) in the truth, in other words, a *continuation* in Christ.

III John: Exhortation About Contributions for Christ. "Beloved, it is a loyal thing you do when you *render any service* to the brethren, . . . You will do well to *send them on their journey* [i.e., pay travel costs]. . . . For they have . . . *accepted nothing* from the heathen. So we ought to *support* such men, that we may be fellow workers in the truth" (5-8). That is, he urges them to make a *contribution* to the cause of Christ.

Jude: Exhortation to Contention for Christ. Jude explained, "I found it necessary to write appealing to you to *contend* for the faith which was once for all delivered to the saints" (3). So his brief letter is an exhortation to put the believers in the sphere of *contention* for Christ against ungodliness (cf. 15) even as Michael was *"contending* with the devil" (9).

So then, in the General Epistles there is an *exhortation* to apply to the believer's life those things about which Paul gave an *exposition* in his epistles. The General Epistles are an application of the truth of Christ *to* the believers, as Paul's letters provided an interpretation of Christ *for* the believers.

Revelation: Consummation in Christ

The last section of the Scriptures is an appropriate climax to all that has preceded it. The Old Testament looked forward to Christ in *anticipation* in that it had laid the foundation for Him (Law), made preparation for Him (History), longed for Him in aspiration (Poetry), and looked for Him in expectation (Prophecy). The New Testament looks on Christ in *realization,* for He has come in a personal manifestation (Gospels), has been the object of evangelization to the world (Acts), the subject of interpretation and application (Epistles) for the believer, and is the One in whom all things will come to a final consummation (Revelation).

In the Gospels, Christ is seen as the *Prophet* to His people; in Acts and the Epistles He is the *Priest* for His people; and in Revelation, Christ is the *King* over His people. First came Christ's incarnation (Gospels), followed by His exaltation (Acts and Epistles), and then His eternal glorification (Revelation). All things were created by Christ (Col. 1:16), in Him all things consist (1:17, ASV), and all things will come to a consummation in Him (1:20). The consummation for all believers in Christ will be salvation (Eph. 1:10).

The consummation for all unbelievers will be subjugation to Christ (Phil. 2:10).

There is perhaps only one unforgivable mistake in interpreting the book of Revelation and that is not to view it Christocentrically. It is above all "the Revelation of Jesus Christ" (1:1). First, it is a revelation of Christ's *person*. Next, it is a revelation of Christ's *possession*, the church which He has purchased with His own blood (1:5). Last, it is a revelation of Christ's *program* (chaps. 4-22) of conquering this world. It looks to the final consummation of human history when "the kingdom of the world has become the kingdom of our Lord and of his Christ" (11:15) and when "the dwelling of God is with men" (21:3).

This chapter began with the thesis that Christ is the underlying theme of each book in the Bible. Now that an attempt has been made to relate every book to Christ, it should be pointed out again that despite the obvious fact that there are many other themes that intermingle with, and sometimes even dominate, the Christocentric theme of a given book, nevertheless, the overall theme of the Bible does not derive its unity from these other strands of truth. Rather, it is only because these strands of truth have been woven into the overall structure of scriptural truth about Christ that they reveal their ultimate meaning. The central meaning of Scripture is Christ, and therefore in a given book it is only the fact that its truth is related to Christ which constitutes that book's significance in relation to the canon of Scripture as a unified whole.

6

THE WORD OF GOD: PERSONAL AND PROPOSITIONAL

Both Christ and the Scriptures are called "the Word of God." The Scriptures are called "the Word of God" as over against the "traditions" of the Jews (Mark 7:13). And in John 10:35 "the word of God" is used as the equivalent of the Old Testament "scripture." The book of Hebrews says "the word of God is living and active" (4:12). Paul refers to the unfailing "word of God" (Rom. 9:6). Acts refers to Paul spending his time "teaching the word of God" (cf. 18:11). There are also some passages in which the Bible is called the "word" (cf. John 17:14, 17; Matt. 13:20) or the "word of truth" (II Tim. 2:15).[1]

In other verses, Christ is referred to as "the word of God" (Rev. 19:13) or "The Word." John wrote in his gospel: "In the beginning was the Word, and the Word was with God, and the Word was God. . . . And the Word became flesh" (John 1:1, 14). In John's first epistle, he said, "That which was from the beginning, which we have heard, which we have seen with our eyes, which we have looked upon and touched with our hands, concerning the *word of life*—the life was made manifest, and we saw it, and testify to it" (1:1-2). John is here bearing witness to Christ, the living word of God, as the preceding verses spoke of the written word of God.

[1]The references in Rev. 1:2, 9; 6:9; 20:4 to the "word of God" may also be of the Bible, but this is not clear.

THE WORD OF GOD

Written	Common Characteristics	Living
II Tim. 3:16	Divine Origin	John 1:1
Heb. 1:1	Human Nature	Heb. 2:14
Rom. 3:2	Jewish Mediation	Heb. 7:14
Ps. 119:138	Faithful	Rev. 19:11
John 17:17	True	John 14:6
John 10:35	Without Error (Sin)	Heb. 4:15
Matt. 5:18	Imperishable	Heb. 1:8
I Peter 1:24-25	Unchangeable	Heb. 13:8
Rom. 1:16*	Power of God	I Cor. 1:24
II Peter 1:4	Precious	I Peter 2:7
Heb. 4:12	Sharp Sword	Rev. 19:15
Ps. 119:105	Light	John 8:12
Luke 4:4 (from Deut. 8:3)	Bread	John 6:51
Ps. 119:129	Wonderful	Isa. 9:6
I Cor. 15:2	Saves	Heb. 7:25
I Tim. 4:5	Sanctifies	I Cor. 1:2
I Peter 1:22	Purifies	Titus 2:14
Ps. 119:9	Cleanses	I John 1:7
Ps. 107:20	Heals	Matt. 4:24
I Peter 2:2	Nourishes	John 6:58
John 8:32	Liberates	Gal. 5:1
Ps. 119:50	Makes Alive	John 5:21
I Peter 1:23	Begets Sons	I Peter 1:3
Matt. 5:18	Lives Forever	Rev. 1:18

*Some of these verses refer to the spoken word of God which later became the written Word of God.

THE SIMILARITY BETWEEN THE LIVING AND WRITTEN WORD

There are some striking parallels between God's living and written Word: between the Saviour and the Scriptures. The comparison on the accompanying chart will illustrate some of these parallels.

It will be noticed that both Christ and Scripture have a dual origin. Christ is at once God and Man in His nature, and the Bible is both divine and human in its origin. That is, the Bible is actually the Word of God but it is also truly the words of men. Furthermore, as Christ is without sin, so the Scriptures are said to be without error. Both are true and unchangeable, and both were given to the world through the Jewish nation.

THE SUPERIORITY OF THE LIVING WORD OVER THE
WRITTEN WORD

Why this close parallel between the Saviour and the Scriptures? Why are the attributes and activities of both so similar? The answers to these questions lie in the nature of what a "Word" of God is, and why God has two of them.

The Word (logos) of God is used at least three ways in the New Testament: (1) as a verbal or oral word from (or about) God (cf. Luke 8:21; Acts 4:31); (2) as the written Word of God (John 10:35; Heb. 4:12, etc.); and (3) as the living Word of God (Christ). In each case, the common *meaning* is in the fact that it is an expression or declaration of God; but the *mode* of expression differs. Since oral and written words differ only as sound differs from symbol, and

THE WORD OF GOD—A DIVINE DECLARATION IN:

Human Language (II Tim. 3:16)	Human Life (I John 1:1)
—Symbols	—A Son (Heb. 1:2)
—Propositions	—A Person (John 14:7)
—A Book	—A Body (Heb. 10:5-7)

since the essence of the oral word of God was reduced to the written Word, the contrast here is basically between two kinds of divine declarations: a written and a living declaration.

HUMAN LIFE OVER HUMAN LANGUAGE

From this comparison it may be seen that God has expressed Himself in two basic ways. First, He has expressed Himself in human language. That which is written (*grapha*) is the Word of God (II Tim. 3:16). That which is written is authoritative, Jesus said (Matt. 5:18 ff.), and it speaks of Him (Luke 24:44). David said, "The Spirit of the LORD speaks by me, his word is upon my tongue" (II Sam. 23:2). Paul speaks of "words not taught by human wisdom but taught by the Spirit" (I Cor. 2:13). That is, the Scriptures are an expression of God's thoughts in man's language.

There is another, and contrasting, revelation of God to man: it is a divine disclosure not in human language but in human life. Since men "share in flesh and blood, he [Christ] himself likewise partook of the same nature" (Heb. 2:14). As John put it, "The Word became flesh and dwelt among us" (John 1:14). There is a certain superiority in this kind of divine expression. Perhaps John explained it best when he said, "We have heard, . . . we have seen with our eyes, . . . we have looked upon and touched with our hands, . . . the word of life" (I John 1:1). That is, the living Word of God is a more perfect expression of God than a written Word, as the presence of a loved one is better than a letter from him. Of course, if the person is absent, then a record of what he desires to communicate is the best that one can expect. So the revelation of God in the Scriptures is essential but the revelation of God in Christ is superior.

THE SON OVER SYMBOLS

Further, the revelation of God in Scripture is one of symbols, for language is a system of symbols. But symbols are only signs or representations of a reality but are not that reality. For example, the symbol *tree*, comprised of four letters, is in no way to be confused with the beautiful evergreen growing in one's yard. Even so, the symbolical expression of God in the Bible should not be confused with God Himself, for this would be bibliolatry (worship of the Bible as divine). God's expression in His *Son* is different from His expression in symbols, for in Christ, the divine Word, there is an identification between God and the expression of God. John said, "The Word [expression of God] *was* God" (John 1:1). Hebrews declares that God "has spoken to us by a *Son*" (1:2) who "reflects the glory of God and bears the very stamp of his nature" (1:3). The revelation of God in His Son is far superior to a revelation in symbols, whether they be types, as the symbols of Old Testament (see chap. 2), or the symbols of human language used in the Bible. The reason is obvious enough: in one case the expression is not to be identified with God (for that would be idolatry) and in the other case it is. In one case there is only a representation of God; in the other there is an identification with God. For John said that Christ the Word is not only the expression of God, but in this unique case, the Word *is* God.

THE PERSONAL OVER THE PROPOSITIONAL

To state the superiority of Christ over the Scriptures in another way, the Scriptures are a propositional revelation, but Christ is a *personal* revelation of God. Of course, there can be propositions about a person, which is precisely what the Scriptures are. But this further supports the point that the person about whom the propositions are written is more important than the propositions themselves. That is, the purpose of the written Word is to convey the Person of the living Word. But, if this is so, then the message of Scripture (viz., person of Christ) is superior to the means of communicating that message (viz., propositions about Christ).

THE BODY OVER THE BOOK

There is another and most obvious superiority of the living Word over the written Word of God mentioned in Hebrews 10:5-7. "When Christ came into the world, he said, '. . . a body hast thou prepared for me; in burnt offerings and sin offerings thou hast taken no pleasure. Then I said, "Lo, I have come to do thy will, O God," as it is written of me in the roll of the book.'" The written Word is a revelation in a book; Christ is the revelation of God in a body—a body which can be a sacrifice for sin. No book can make expiation for sin, as did "the offering of the body of Jesus Christ once for all" (Heb. 10:10, cf. Rom. 3:25). It was not ink but blood which was necessary for man's salvation (Heb. 9:22). The book can give a revelation of God, but only the body and blood of Christ can bring about a reconciliation to God (II Cor. 5:18-21).

From these contrasts it should be evident that God's revelation in Christ is superior to His revelation in Scripture. Christ is not only superior by way of redemption but by way of being a higher kind of revelation. For as one is compared to the other, Christ is more important than Scripture in the same way in which a man's life is more important than language about him (e.g., in a biography). Jesus said the Scriptures were "concerning himself" (Luke 24:27), or they were "written about me" (v. 44), or "it is written of me" (Heb. 10:7), or they "bear witness to me" (John 5:39). In each case the purpose and consequent value of the written Word is that it conveys the living Word of God;[2] the resulting importance of the propositions about Christ is that they reveal the person of Christ. In this sense then, Christ is superior to Scripture because He is more important than the statements about Himself. Inasmuch as the Scriptures then are revelatory of Christ, one should not reverence the

[2]This is not to say that the Word of God could have no antecedent or intrinsic value in itself if it did not reveal Christ. The Word of God would have value no matter *what* it said because of *who* said it, viz., God who is the ultimate source of all value.

words of the Bible themselves, but rather, he should respect them for Christ's sake—because they speak of Him.

The Necessity of the Written Word

If the written Word is inferior to the living Word as a means of revealing God, then why did Christ vest it with such authority (see chap. 1)? Why did Jesus Himself so often take His stand upon the authority of the written Word (cf. Matt. 4:4 ff.; 5:17-18; Mark 7:6-8)? Why are the Scriptures referred to as divinely inspired (II Tim. 3:16), unbreakable (John 10:35), and imperishable (Matt. 5:18)? Why is there such a close parallel between the attributes and activities of the written and living Word (see chart on p. 112)?

The Living Word Is More Important Than the Written Word

The Bible is not a "paper pope." It is not in itself divine; it should not be worshiped. The Bible is not God; it consists of human words *through* which God speaks. It is the *Word* of God, but it is expressed in the *words* of men. Christ, on the other hand, *is* God (John 1:1; Heb. 1:8) and should be worshiped (Heb. 1:6; John 5:23). And so the parallel between the Bible and Christ is not perfect. It is a mistake to view the *inspiration* of the written Word and the *incarnation* of the living Word as perfect parallels. It is not correct to consider the sense in which God declares Himself in the propositions of Scripture the same as the sense in which God dwells in the person of His Son. The finite, limited words of the Bible only provide a *definition* of God's essence, whereas Christ, being God, gives a *demonstration* of it.

An analogy may be drawn from the revelation of God in nature. God is revealed *through* creation (Rom. 1:20; Ps. 19:1 ff.), but God is not to be identified *with* creation in any of its forms—this is idolatry (Rom. 1:21-23). In like manner, God is revealed *through* the Bible, but He should not be identified *with* the Bible— this is bibliolatry.

Jesus rebuked the Jews for identifying the words of the Bible with the source of eternal life. They thought they could find spiritual life *within* the words of the Old Testament. Jesus said, "Ye do (indeed) search the Scriptures . . . for in them [not *through* them, as a mere means to get at the living word of God] ye imagine to have eternal life; and they are they which testify of Me. And [yet—how inconsistent, how preposterous!] ye are not willing to come to Me that ye might have [that eternal] life" (John 5:39-40).[3] They knew the shell of Scripture but ignored the soul. They searched superstitiously through the symbols of Scripture as though they were sacred, and missed the Saviour about whom these symbols spoke. Jesus said, "If you believed Moses, you would believe me, for he wrote of me," and "yet you refuse to come to me that you may have life" (John 5:46, 40). Eternal life is found *in* Christ and only *through* the Bible. The incarnation is the manifestation of that life (John 1:4), and inspiration is the means by which we have an authoritative record of it (II Peter 1:20-21).

THE WRITTEN WORD IS IMPORTANT TO THE LIVING WORD

This is far from saying that the authority of the Bible is unimportant or that the Scriptures have no essential value but only an instrumental value (insofar as they convey Christ). It is only to say that when the Bible and Christ are compared as two modes of God's revelation, the reality of Christ is more important than the authority of the Bible.[4]

INSPIRATION IS IMPORTANT AS AN EXPRESSION OF GOD

As a matter of fact, the Scriptures are valuable not merely because they are a revelation about Someone (viz., Christ), but also because they are a revelation of and from Someone

[3]As translated by John Lange, *Commentary on the Holy Scriptures: John* (Grand Rapids: Zondervan), IX, 195.

[4]For example, men were saved before there was a Bible (as Abraham), and no doubt men are saved today without having a Bible (e.g., through a verbal testimony or tract), but no one is ever saved apart from the work of Christ (I Tim. 2:5; John 14:6).

(viz., God). Whatever God expresses is of value, because He is the source and substance of value Himself (cf. James 1:17: I John 4:7-8). And since the Scriptures are the Word or expression of God, they are valuable as such, regardless of their content or theme. That is, *what* the Bible says is important because of *who* said it.

And not only is the Bible important because of who said it, but it is inerrant (without error) for the same reason. For God cannot utter a lie (Heb. 6:18) or make an error (Ps. 18:30). And since the Scriptures are an utterance of God (II Tim. 3:16; II Peter 1:20-21), then it follows that they are true and without error in all that they teach. As Jesus said, the "scripture cannot be broken" (John 10:35), and "till heaven and earth pass away, not an iota, not a dot, will pass from the law until all is accomplished" (Matt. 5:18).

INSPIRATION IS IMPORTANT FOR THE PROPAGATION OF CHRIST

Furthermore, the Scriptures have value not only because they are an expression of God or even because they are an expression about Christ, but because they are a suitable means for the propagation and preservation of this truth.

Of course God could have chosen some other way to preserve and propagate His truth than in a book. As a matter of fact, in time past God spoke "in many and various ways . . . to our fathers by the prophets" (Heb. 1:1). God sometimes spoke through (1) angels (Gen. 19); (2) dreams (Gen. 37); (3) visions (Dan. 7:1); (4) miracles (Judges 6:37); (5) a voice (I Sam. 3:4 ff.), (6) nature (Ps. 19:1), etc. God could have continued to reveal Himself in these ways, but He did not so limit Himself. Instead, He chose to have His revelation recorded in the words of Scripture, perhaps for the same reason men record their words in books today, that is, it is a more precise way to preserve and propagate them.

Another alternative to a written preservation of truth is an oral tradition or continuation of it. However, oral tradition tends to be easily perverted, as anyone knows who has ever traced a tale through the "grapevine" of oral communications. An oral tradition from the lips of Christ was once perverted within the circle of His apostles who heard Him say that John *may not* die before Christ returned. This they misinterpreted to mean John *would not* die (John 21:23-24).[5] If an oral statement was perverted from the lips of Christ to the ears of His apostles, how much more would distortion occur down through the chain of the centuries. The preservation and propagation of truth is more readily attained in a written than in oral form. Men know this, and it was only appropriate that God too should use this means to preserve and propagate His Word.

INSPIRATION IS IMPORTANT TO THE INTERPRETATION OF CHRIST

However, it is not only the propagation but also the interpretation of Christ that is at stake in His relation to Scripture. It has been argued throughout this book that Christ is the key to the interpretation of the Scriptures (cf. chap. 2). If it is true that the Bible speaks about Christ, then what it says about Christ is very important, and it is supremely important whether or not what it says is true. It is this fact that makes the authority and authenticity of the Bible a very important issue. For if the Bible does not give an authoritative and authentic interpretation of Christ, as it claims to give, then it is an erring and fallible one; and how can one be certain about Christ if all he has is an uncertain word about Christ? (Cf. I Cor. 14:8.)

One's understanding of the living Word, upon whom he depends for eternal life (cf. John 8:24), is limited to the channel through which that truth is mediated to him, namely, the written Word. Granted that the Bible is only a medium through which God speaks, even so, one's knowledge of Christ is channeled through that medium. If the channel is imperfect and erring, so one's knowledge of Christ will be

[5]That the apostles could be wrong on something they *personally believed* does not contradict the truth that they could not err in any doctrine they *officially taught* (cf. John 14:26; 16:13).

imperfect and erring. Even if the propositional truth is viewed simply as the instrument of conveying the personal revelation, nevertheless one's knowledge of the Person which it presents will be no better than the propositions which present Him. To use another example, an imperfect or scratched record of the most perfectly performed symphony will utter a very imperfect sound. So the sufficiency of one's knowledge of the person of Christ is limited to the adequacy of the record which conveys that Person to him. For the sufficiency of one's knowledge about Christ is no better than the veracity of the record which brings Christ to him.

Of course, one may argue that the Bible is without error when it speaks about the "spiritual" things which relate to Christ, but that it is not errorless on historical, factual or nondoctrinal issues. However, there are two basic problems with this in view: (1) In many cases it is impossible to separate the historical from the spiritual. What can the virgin birth mean if Mary committed adultery? If it is not a biological and historical fact, then it is a theological fiction as well. What can the crucifixion signify if there was no blood-stained cross? It is senseless to speak of the resurrection of Christ unless His body supernaturally and permanently vacated Joseph's tomb (cf. I Cor. 15:17). (2) Further, one's confidence in the doctrines which are not directly related to historical data (e.g., heaven, immortality), is necessarily conditioned by those that are. For how can one trust the Scripture on matters which are not factually or historically verifiable if it is proven in error on matters which have been objectively treated? To borrow the words of Jesus, "If I have told you earthly things and you do not believe, how can you believe if I tell you of heavenly things?" (John 3:12).

One is not wrong in considering the written Word to be an errorless record about Christ, for Jesus said, "Scripture cannot be broken" (John 10:35). And again, "Truly, I say to you, till heaven and earth pass away, not an iota, not a dot, will pass from the law until all is accomplished" (Matt.

5:18). Now it is sufficient to say that if Jesus verified the flawless nature of the Old Testament which revealed Him only by way of anticipation, that the New Testament is an equally errorless record of the even more important manifestation and interpretation of Christ.

Both Christ and Scripture are revelations. As expressions of God, both have essential value. Since, however, it is the primary purpose of Scripture to point to Christ, the latter is more important than the former. But inasmuch as one's picture of Christ is no better than the portrait painted in Scripture, each stroke of divine truth is very important to one's overall impression of Christ. As a consequence of this, the Christian can be satisfied to know that wherever he turns in the Bible he finds his Lord.

> I find my Lord in the Bible
>   Where ever I chance to look,
> He is the theme of the Bible
>   The center and heart of the Book;
> He is the Rose of Sharon,
>   He is the Lily fair,
> Where ever I open my Bible
>   The Lord of the Book is there.
>
> He, at the Book's beginning,
>   Gave to the earth its form,
> He is the Ark of shelter
>   Bearing the brunt of the storm,
> The Burning Bush of the desert,
>   The budding of Aaron's Rod,
> Where ever I look in the Bible
>   I see the Son of God.
>
> The Ram upon Mt. Moriah,
>   The Ladder from earth to sky,
> The Scarlet Cord in the window,
>   And the Serpent lifted high,
> The smitten rock in the desert,
>   The Shepherd with staff and crook,

The face of my Lord I discover
  Where ever I open the Book.

He is the Seed of the Woman,
  The Savior Virgin-born;
He is the Son of David,
  Whom men rejected with scorn,
His garments of grace and of beauty
  The stately Aaron deck,
Yet He is a priest forever,
  For He is Melchizedek.

Lord of eternal glory
  Whom John, the Apostle saw;
Light of the golden city,
  Lamb without spot or flaw,
Bridegroom coming at midnight,
  For whom the Virgins look.
Where ever I open my Bible,
  I find my Lord in the Book.

AUTHOR UNKNOWN

BIBLIOGRAPHY

HODGKIN, A. M. *Christ in All the Scripture*. London: Pickering & Inglis, 1922. This is a devotionally oriented, comprehensive survey of the types and pictures of Christ in every book of the Bible. Pp. 249, including a topical index.

LIGHTNER, ROBERT. *The Savior and the Scriptures*. Philadelphia: Presbyterian & Reformed, 1966. Originally his doctoral dissertation on Jesus' use of the Old Testament, defending the divine origin and inspiration of the Scriptures against contemporary denials. Pp. 170, footnotes and indexes.

LOWE, MARMION L. *Christ in All the Scriptures*. Bible School Park, Broome Co., N.Y.: pub. privately, 1954. This is a highly technological study of the offices, names and attributes of Christ throughout the Bible. Pp. 130, no index.

MORGAN, G. CAMPBELL. *The Unfolding Message of the Bible*. Westwood, N. J.: Revell, 1961. An informal unfolding of the divine harmony of the whole Bible in the person and history of Christ. Pp. 416, no notes or index.

SAPHIR, A. *Christ and the Scriptures*. New York: Gospel Pub., n.d. A presentation of the testimony of Christ and the apostles to the inspiration of the Bible, with a comparison between the written and living Word of God. Pp. 142.

———. *The Divine Unity of Scriptures*. Los Angeles: Biola, 8th ed., n.d. Lectures on the organic unity of the Bible by a Jewish Presbyterian, stressing both the unity and authority of the Scriptures over against the rationalism of his day. The approach is apologetical and more theologically than Christocentrically related. Pp. 304, no notes, references or index.

SCROGGIE, W. G. *Christ the Key to Scripture*. Chicago: Bible Inst. Colportage Assn., 1924. A brief but good structural approach which traces Christ throughout the Bible. Pp. 47, no notes or index.

WENHAM, J. W. *Our Lord's View of the Old Testament*. London: Tyndale, 1953. Pp. 32. This is a very fine little summary of Jesus' view of the authority and authenticity of the Old Testament, with Scripture passages and a brief discussion of some of the problems. No bibliography or index.

SUBJECT INDEX

SCRIPTURE INDEX

126